What It Means
to Be a Man

What It Means to Be a Man

Reflections on Puerto Rican Masculinity

Rafael L. Ramírez
Translated by Rosa E. Casper

Rutgers University Press

New Brunswick, New Jersey, and London

First published in Spanish in 1993 as *Dime Capitán: Reflexiones sobre la Masculinidad,* by Ediciones Huracán, Rio Piedras, Puerto Rico
First published in English in 1999 by Rutgers University Press, New Brunswick, New Jersey

Library of Congress Cataloging-in-Publication Data

Ramírez, Rafael L.
    [Dime capitán. English]
    What it means to be a man : reflections on Puerto Rican
masculinity / Rafael L. Ramírez ; translated by Rosa E. Casper.
      p. cm.
    First published in Spanish as "Dime capitán : reflexiones sobre
la masculinidad," 1993.
    Includes bibliographical references and index.
    ISBN 0-8135-2660-4 (hardcover : alk. paper). —
ISBN 0-8135-2661-2 (pbk. : alk. paper)
    1. Masculinity—Puerto Rico. 2. Machismo—Puerto Rico.
3. Sexism—Puerto Rico. I. Casper, Rosa E. II. Title.
BF692.5.R3513 1999
  155.3'32'097295—dc21   98-49682
                                                   CIP

British Cataloging-in-Publication data for this book is available from the British Library

Manufactured in the United States of America

Contents

Foreword

At the 1996 meeting of the American Ethnological Society in Puerto Rico, I participated, along with Dr. Rafael L. Ramírez, in a panel entitled "The Politics of Person, Identity, and Emotion in Puerto Rico." During that meeting, the American Ethnological Society recognized Dr. Ramírez as one of the "Pioneers of Puerto Rican Anthropology." In his paper at the session, Dr. Ramírez made the crucial observation that while men as a class are powerful in Puerto Rico (and in many other societies), we should recognize that all men are not equally powerful, nor are all women equally subordinated. In particular, the fissures of social class, gender identity, and sexual orientation create inequalities in access to power and give rise to marked heterogeneities in the social positions of both men and women. This point is masterfully developed in *What It Takes to Be a Man: Reflections on Puerto Rican Masculinity*.

One of the most important contributions of *What It Takes to Be a Man* is its thorough deconstruction of the concept of "machismo." Tracing the genesis of the term to the social science literature of the 1950s and 1960s, Ramírez makes clear that this concept, popularized in the literature on population control in Puerto Rico, was imposed on, and did not grow out of, the Latino experience. He draws important distinctions between the role of the macho, the positive and negative valences of "masculinity" in Puerto Rican culture, and the caricature of "machismo" that has evolved in the social science literature. Moreover, by critiquing the mistaken assumption that attitudes and behaviors associated with "machismo" are a lower-class phenomenon, he offers profound insights into the ways in which social definitions of masculinity vary. While the expressions of the macho role are shaped by social class and status, Ramírez identifies common threads of expression and behavior that run through Puerto Rican men's expressions of their gender identities.

One of the most creative and entertaining chapters of the book, "We the Boricuas," discusses the social construction of "masculinity" in Puerto Rico through analysis of the colorful and richly layered slang used in a wide range of everyday interactions. Ramírez demonstrates how these expressions both reflect and enact gendered power relationships in Puerto Rico. This play of highly symbolic language is charged with issues of sexuality and power. Ramírez demonstrates how the language of sexuality—be it in poetry or in a bar, in university protests or in political backrooms—is used to mark power and subordination. The creativity of the chapter emerges in the ways that Ramírez takes common phrases and, through careful analysis, expands the reader's awareness of the complexity of meanings in these terms.

"The Homosexual Question" (Chapter 4) thoughtfully examines the differing ways in which sexual identity and sexual activity in Puerto Rico are structured and contrasts these patterns with constructions of sexual identity in the United States. After a brief orienting section defining homosexuality and analyzing differing perspectives on the construction of homosexuality, Ramírez returns to linguistic analyses in his discussion of *el ambiente*, the world of homosexuality in Puerto Rico. He uses linguistic analyses to demonstrate how power is deployed against Puerto Rican homosexuals and to illuminate the pain engendered by this discrimination. For example, the term used in Puerto Rico to refer to the penetrated partner in homosexual sex is *loca*, which is a term also used to refer to those who are crazy and whose mental illness is most out of control and most hopeless. He points out that the Gay Pride Community of San Juan has substituted the English "gay" for more pejorative terms like *loca*. It is striking that to move out of the pejorative position marked by *la loca* requires a code switch from Spanish to English.

The concluding chapter calls for a search for a "new masculinity" and for a renewed effort to move forward in reconstructing masculinity. Ramírez sees the answer to the problem of constructing a "new masculinity" in the "New Age" neither in a search for the Wild Man nor in a movement to atone for being a man and therefore an oppressor. Rather, he argues that through careful analysis and understanding of the fact that issues of power pervade the dynamics of gender relations, creative and honest efforts to change such dynamics can and must be forged in Puerto Rico and in all societies.

It is a great pleasure for me to have been involved with Rutgers University Press in the process of making this important work on masculinity accessible to an English-speaking audience. This book, by one of Puerto Rico's most distinguished anthropologists, is important for the English-speaking public to read and engage. Too often, constructions of "masculinity" in Puerto Rico and other Latino societies have been understood by outsiders only through poorly defined and pejorative concepts like "machismo." Further, by opening the analysis of gender to masculine identities, *What It Takes to Be a Man* represents an important contribution to the field of gender studies.

This book combines the insight and sensitivity of an insider to Puerto Rican culture with the skill and acumen of one of the most important anthropologists of his generation to suggest new approaches to understanding masculinity, both in Puerto Rico and more widely.

—Peter J. Guarnaccia

Translator's

Note

Given that the subject of the book is the construction of masculinity in Puerto Rico, which has been related through the use of slang terms, regionalisms, and expressions in Spanish, the text is translated in a way that preserves the examples for the non-Spanish reader. Readability is an important factor. Since there are many endnotes in the source text, no additional footnotes are added to explain the previous concepts. Therefore, the reader will find an indirect explanation, approximation, or literal translation in parentheses next to each Spanish term.

In most cases, there is a U.S. equivalent or explanation next to the idea. If the idea had already been explained in the preceding pages, the term is left untouched.

There are, however, a few terms that have been maintained in Spanish because they are concepts that have been studied and are of such widespread use that they have been incorporated into the U.S. language and appear in U.S. dictionaries. The two most obvious examples are the words "machismo" and "macho," but in the first endnote in the first chapter, the Mexican terminology for *charros, rancheras*, and *corridos* has been kept, since they are subjects of study.

Similarly, in chapter 3 of the book, "We the Boricuas,"
Dr. Ramírez has included a verse from the poem "Majestad
Negra" by Luis Palés Matos. Children in Puerto Rico study
and learn this poem in school. Whether children realize it
or not, this piece of history becomes ingrained, a part of
their being, since they learn it at a young age. This refrain
not only eroticizes the black woman but also represents
the harvest of sugarcane, once very vital to Puerto Rico's
economy. Below is the poem in its entirety:

Majestad Negra
Por la encendida calle antillana
va Tembandumba de la Quimbamba
—Rumba, macumba, candombe, bámbula—
entre dos filas de negras caras.
Ante ella un congo—gongo y maraca—
ritma una conga bomba que bamba.

Culipandeando la Reina avanza
y de su inmensa grupa resbalan
meneos cachondos que el gongo cuaja
en ríos de azúcar y de melaza.
Prieto trapiche de sensual zafra,
el caderamen, masa con masa,
exprime ritmos, suda que sangra,
y la molienda culmina en danza.

Por la encendida calle antillana
va Tembandumba de la Quimbamba.
Flor de Tortola, rosa de Uganda,
por ti crepitan bombas y bámbulas;
por ti en calendas desenfrenadas
quema la Antilla su sangre ñáñiga.

Haití te ofrece sus calabazas;
fogososos rones te da Jamaica;
Cuba te dice: ¡dale, mulata!
Y Puerto Rico: ¡melao, melamba!

¡Sús, mis cocolos de negras caras!
Tronad, tambores; vibrad, maracas.
Por la encendida calle antillana
—Rumba, macumba, candombe, bámbula—
va Tembandumba de la Quimbamba.

In this piece of poetry, Palés Matos incorporated African words (*Tembandumba*), played with words (*rumba, macumba, candombe, bámbula*), and created uncommon usage for common words (turning *ritmo* into a verb), all formulated in decasyllabic meter with a particular rhyme scheme and acoustic pattern. In the stanza used in the book, the reader of Spanish can feel the rhythm (as in the first line, "Culipandeando la Reina avanza") and see the images ("meneos cachondos") that Palés Matos describes. In the translation, the Spanish verse is printed with a version in English below it, allowing the reader to "hear" and "see" how this large black woman is walking down the street to the beat of various percussion instruments.

From the meter arises the rhythm of the verse. The translation intends to re-create a rhythm as Palés Matos did in Spanish—to the sound of a steady beat. Alliteration has been used to help create this rhythm, as Palés Matos used. He used assonance at the end of words, such as *inmen**sa** grup**a** res**balan**; men**eos** cach**ondos**; and *el gon**go** cua**ja***. Although every syllable begins with a consonant in Spanish, the reader should note that the final sound of the words mainly ends in vowels. Palés Matos also used consonant alliteration:

sensual zafra and *suda que sangre*. The last two examples place more stress on the first part of the word, so the alliteration works well. In the English translation, alliteration and one- and two-syllable words try to achieve a similar effect: "sexy shimmy moves"; "sugar—sweet and brown"; and "cane crop."

Part of Palés Matos's strong imagery arises from his masterly use of meter and rhythm. He chose his words so well that the reader of Spanish can hear the percussion and see the woman walking. Words such as *culipandeando, inmensa grupa, meneos cachondos,* and *masa con masa* all contribute to the image of a very wide-hipped swinging woman with large buttocks. In the translation, terms such as "large backside," "avalanche of sexy shimmy moves," and "baby-making hips" have been used to convey that largeness. With respect to "hearing" the beats, "rhythms beat down" and "squeezing out the rhythms" are intended to give the sense of the music, and reading the poem out loud contributes to a rhythmical beat.

—Rosa E. Casper

Acknowledgments

A sabbatical leave from the University of Puerto Rico, Río Piedras Campus, allowed me to dedicate 1992 to writing this book. The Institutional Fund for Research (FIPI, its acronym in Spanish) contributed the funds for the research on the literature of machismo. Friends and colleagues supported me throughout the process. I am very grateful to those who commented on and criticized the text: Idsa E. Alegría Ortega, Juan José Baldrich, Ineke Cunningham, Jaime de la Cruz, Jaime Díaz Alemany, Arturo Fernández Ortiz, Juan G. Gelpí, José Ramón Ortiz, and Eduardo Rivera Medina.

—Rafael L. Ramírez

What It Means
to Be a Man

Introduction

My first encounter with the term "machismo" occurred many years ago when I registered for my first and only sociology course, which I attended for only a few weeks. In my brief encounter with the class, I remember only the professor's emphasis on the concepts of socialization and of machismo as characteristic of the Puerto Rican male. I found the latter concept curious but did not give it much thought. At that time, my contact with the social sciences was minimal: it consisted of the basic course that was a requirement for all undergraduate students of the University of Puerto Rico and a psychology course, a requirement of the college in which I studied. Neither of these courses spoke of machismo. In the university or in the Puerto Rico of that era, I was also never exposed to a questioning of the attributes, responsibilities, and privileges of masculinity.

Many months after my limited exposure to sociology, I began my graduate studies in anthropology, during which I read the texts of that time that dealt with machismo as a subject. Machismo was presented as a Latin American phenomenon that was most notably manifested among lower-class men. I also listened to comments by my classmates, who considered machismo to be exotic, an indicator of "underdevelopment," a phenomenon foreign to the culture of the United States. I was not impressed by the texts, nor did I see myself reflected in what was said by the sociologists or my classmates. This was possibly due to the fact that in my socialization as a Puerto Rican male, the emphasis had been on the obligations of masculinity, on the responsibilities involved in being a man, and particularly on being the provider and breadwinner for others. In my particular case, emphasis was placed on the fact that being the oldest son, and the first grandson of my paternal grandparents, I was expected to assume the responsibility—when the time came—for the well-being of my brother, sister, father, mother, grandfather, and grandmothers. In my family and my friends' families, sexuality was not discussed, and womanizers, gamblers, drunks, and irresponsible men were criticized. Two alcoholic uncles by marriage caused much suffering and shame, and they were considered a bad example. They were a daily sign of what one should not be.

During my time as a graduate student in the United States, Latin American machismo was a behavior distant to me, although I did know about the sexual adventures of some of the Hispanic students who liked to play the role of Latin lovers. For them, all American women were whores, and it was a matter of *culearse las cabras* (getting a piece), as a Chilean friend of mine would say. In my opinion, his behavior and attitudes toward women seemed similar to the Americans'. With respect to the qualities of masculinity, he did not notice any differences between the behaviors of the Latin Americans and the Americans he knew and with whom he interacted, mostly students and professors. At first, I was struck by the fact that the American men of the university world were less brusque in dealing with others than were Puerto Rican men and did not touch their genitals in public. In my ignorance, I considered this to be a cultural trait, when in reality it was class behavior. At that time, I also did not recognize what I now see as the discourses of masculinity. In any case, references to our machismo seemed to me to be anecdotal—unproven facts and affirmations lacking scientific validity.

While doing field research for my doctoral dissertation, I became very removed from the university environment, which I had entered when I was sixteen years old. For a year, my contact with the university was limited to two days a week when I taught classes. I spent the rest of the time living in a municipality of the San Juan metropolitan area, researching the political behavior of those who lived in shantytowns and public housing. Given that political behavior was the central topic of my research, I had to grapple with the study of power relations and their expressions within the context of the local party structures and daily life. Additionally, the fact that a large part of the party leadership in the neighborhoods was composed of men necessitated that I interact with them in different scenarios and observe their communications and conflicts. In my mind and in my research designs, masculinity was not included, and I did not even remember the term "machismo." It was not used by the people in the neighborhoods that I studied, although there were constant references to "being a man." One night, upon returning home after conducting many interviews, I heard a heated discussion between two men, and I went toward the balcony to observe them. In the altercation, each one stressed that he was more of a macho than the other and demanded respect. At that, I remembered machismo and wrote it down in my diary to study it in the future.

Approximately nine years after I witnessed this incident,

I began to read the academic literature on machismo as groundwork for a comparative study. At that time—the end of the seventies—the term was very widespread in the academic world of Puerto Rico and in feminist criticism. The director of the Anthropology Department at Harvard helped me and facilitated my access to the archives that we anthropologists know as the "Human Relations Area File," where I began my search. To my surprise, information on machismo was minimal, and it came from anthropological studies in Mexico and Puerto Rico with which I was already familiar. I searched under "masculinity" and found descriptions of masculine behavior in societies in which the term "machismo" was not used. I then realized that the aim of my study was masculinity, not machismo. As I began to read studies on masculinity, I found Dover's book (1978) on homosexuality in ancient Greece, which confirmed my conjecture that the distinguishing feature of masculinity lies in its principles of power.

When I was prepared to write up the results of my readings in the literature on machismo, I received a call from Víctor de la Cancela, a Puerto Rican who was finishing a detailed study of the literature on machismo for his doctoral dissertation and had heard that I was studying the subject. We had a meeting in which we exchanged bibliographies and discussed our respective studies. Since we agreed on our criticisms of the literature, it did not make sense that I write a review of all that literature. I concentrated my efforts on reading and analyzing investigations and other publications on masculinity.

The purpose of this book is to explore the construction of masculinity in Puerto Rico and to share my thoughts concerning what it means to be a man. It is also an invitation to Puerto Ricans to begin a process of introspection and dialogue about our subjectivity and to contemplate the possibility of transforming it. This book begins with a critique of the uses of the term "machismo" and of its uncritical application both by men and in some feminist discourses (chapter 1).

Chapter 2 analyzes masculinity as a social construction. From an anthropological perspective, I describe the constructionist approach to gender studies and present the diversity in the expressions of masculinity based on ethnographic studies.

In chapter 3, I present my interpretation of what it means to be a Puerto Rican man. I embark upon the discussion of the attributes and demands of our masculinity, pointing out the elements we share: power, competition, and sexuality in conjunction with power and pleasure.

Chapter 4 deals with erotic relationships between men as part of the expressions of masculinity and analyzes how the homosexual environment reproduces the dominant masculine ideology.

Finally, in chapter 5, I present the possibility of constructing a new masculinity, liberated from the power games that characterize Puerto Rican men. Rather than giving answers, I formulate questions geared toward responding to the challenge that the women's movement has issued to us. The women's movement has argued with much success for the transformation of gender relationships and a new conceptualization of the feminine; it has also made us see that now is the time to enact changes.

The chapters and sections constitute essays in and of themselves, linked by the concepts of power and of gender as a social construction. In this book, power is not considered an attribute restricted to a few who treasure and preserve it. On the contrary, I propose that power is an integral part of all of our relationships, and I consider men to be participants in cycles of authority and rebellion. What I have written is not the result of field research, a survey, or an empirical study. Nor is it autobiographical. The book is a contemplation that arises out of observations and experiences, and out of introspection into my Puerto Rican male subjectivity. It is an interpretation in search of the meanings of masculinity within the approaches of interpretative anthropology and anthropology as cultural criticism (Clifford and Marcus 1986; Marcus and Fischer 1986). From an interpretative perspective, I use Geertz's metaphor (1973) that culture is like a text in which social actions can be read in terms of their meanings. Likewise, I support the recognition that social life is fundamentally a negotiation of meanings (Marcus and Fischer 1986, 26).

1

Machismo

We men, especially those who are Latin American, are commonly described as *machistas,* and our behaviors are cataloged under the category known as "machismo." To a large extent, we are categorized as beings who are aggressive, oppressive, narcissistic, insecure, loudmouthed, womanizers, massive drinkers, persons who have an uncontrollable sexual prowess, and who are, as Jorge Negrete would sing, *parranderos de parranda larga* (don't-stop-'til-you-drop partiers).[1]

"Machismo," a term that presumes to be a concept, was popularized in the social literature of the fifties and sixties and was initially presented as a Latin American phenomenon that appeared in its crudest form in the peasant and working classes.[2] The ethnocentric and class natures of the first approaches to the literature on machismo—ethnocentric because of its emphasis on what is Latin American and classist because machismo behavior is situated almost exclusively in certain social classes—were modified when machismo was incorporated into feminist discourse and into the daily speech of men and women in Latin America and the United States (Stone 1974). Although many authors (Abad, Ramos, and Boyce 1974; Padilla and Ruiz 1973) pointed out some purportedly positive aspects of machismo, such as courage, responsibility, and perseverance, the fact remains that the term is associated with male traits or behaviors to which negative qualities are attributed: "the sum total of simultaneous brutality, arrogance, and submissiveness" (De Jesús Guerrero 1977, 37). In addition, the term has been incorporated into the repertoire of insults along with "barbarian, savage, gorilla, lout, and *cafre* (Kaffir)."[3]

Examining the literature on machismo, we find the term used in multiple ways: sometimes as a set of attitudes, other times as a configuration of traits, and still other times as a syndrome. These are the frames of reference that specify the individual characteristics. In the abundant literature, there is a great deal of repetition in the definitions and descriptions. It can be said that most of the documents on machismo are variations of the initial approaches by Bermúdez (1955) and Stycos (1955). Bermúdez defines machismo as a typical case of unconscious compensation against feminist tendencies hidden in the Mexican man. From Bermúdez on, a current of thinking develops that perceives machismo as an intrapsychic phenomenon dissociated from its sociohistorical roots. This current continued to examine machismo from the perspective of psychology, describing it in a language categorized by clinical interpretations and opinions and paying inadequate attention to historical processes, social structures, and cultural categories.

In a study whose principal aim is exploring the social dynamics of demographic growth and the forms in which culture "in part determines the circumstances under which, and the extent to which, coitus occurs" (8), Stycos explains machismo as an analytical category. In other words, Stycos is studying sociocultural aspects of human fertility in order to make specific recommendations to guide the Puerto Rican birth control programs of the fifties, and among the obstacles to lowering the birthrate, Stycos stresses machismo. What does he understand "machismo" to mean?

> The drive in males to manifest their virility we have termed *machismo*. The complex would not seem to have the importance, ascribed to it before the field investigation, of driving men to produce a limitless quantity of children. However, it may have other direct and indirect effects on fertility: (1) the anxiety to disprove sterility encourages a rapid first birth; (2) the anxiety over production of male offspring, to prove that one can "make males," may encourage higher fertility where female offspring occur earlier in birth order; (3) serial marriage and extramarital activity may be partly products of a need to demonstrate sexuality; (4) certain negative attitudes toward birth control seem related to this complex. For example, resistance to the condom in the way of preference for the "clean spur" (*espuela limpia*) might be interpreted as a product of a virility-manifesting drive. (246)

For Stycos, "machismo" means virility, and as evidence he offers the responses of 72 men to the following questions: "Speaking of being a *macho completo* (complete man), how does a man show it? How does he prove it?" Of those interviewed, 15.4 percent answered that machismo is manifested "through abusiveness." The percentage of answers associated with what some have called the positive aspects of machismo (courage, honesty, chivalry, reliability, being a good neighbor, and being man of honor) was 73.7 percent, while those associated with virility and sexuality came to 39.2 percent.[4] Despite the fact that the results of the survey do not prove that the set of attitudes he calls "machismo" is responsible for a man's wanting to have many children, Stycos emphasizes those answers associated with sexuality in order to conclude that machismo is a "general lower-class value" (42) and is transmitted by penis adulation of infants and by the reinforcement of activities considered to be masculine. Describing the socialization process that turns the *machito en macho* (little male into a male), he notes:

> The most striking manifestation of attempts to inculcate *machismo* occurs in the adult adulation of the infantile penis. By praising and calling a great deal of attention to the penis, the parent can communicate to the child the literal or symbolic value of the male organ. (42)

Stycos arrives at this conclusion, and he acknowledges this, by quoting out of context from ethnographic reports. By concentrating on the study of lower classes, he does not realize that penis adulation is a generalized phenomenon in Puerto Rico and is seen in all social classes. On the other hand, because he lacks a historical and comparative perspective, Stycos does not recognize that such behavior forms part of phallocentrism or the penis cult that characterizes many societies in which the masculine ideology is dominant. Therefore, it is not specific or exclusive to a few Puerto Ricans.[5]

In later research, Hill, Stycos, and Back (1959) focused on what is known as the "machismo complex," which was subjected to verification in a new survey administered to 322 Puerto Rican men. Analysis of the results showed that in the men surveyed, there existed no unconscious anxieties that might lead them to prove their virility. Hill, Stycos, and Back are emphatic in their position with respect to machismo:

The alleged masculinity drives, which are supposed to lie behind the Puerto Rican male's opposition to family limitation, appear largely the figment of [the imagination of] novelists and others who have stereotyped all Puerto Rican men with the *macho* stamp. In Puerto Rico men are authoritarian, dominant, and distant, but not virility obsessed. (375)

This finding seems to have no impact on the subsequent definitions of machismo. Almost two decades later, Stevens and other researchers point out that machismo is an orientation, which she describes as the "cult of virility."

The chief characteristics of this cult are exaggerated aggressiveness and intransigence in male-to-male interpersonal relationships and arrogance and sexual aggression in male-to-female relationships. (Stevens 1976, 90)

In the range of definitions of machismo, many variations and subtleties are incorporated according to the conceptualizations or purposes of those who write about the subject. As a general rule, the literature on machismo is essentially descriptive, uncritical, and repetitive. The term is invariably defined as a set of attitudes, behaviors, and practices that characterize men. Some authors pay more attention to individual psychological characteristics and point out the traits of immaturity, narcissism, having an inferiority complex, aggressiveness, promiscuity, irresponsibility, latent homosexuality, ambivalence toward and conflictive relationships with women, and sexual anxiety. There is, therefore, a tendency to focus on machismo on the individual level, emphasizing machismo's pathological and destructive aspects; that is to say, a position framed within a clinical discourse.

Others approach the study of machismo from what can be called a sociocultural perspective, because it focuses more on social, economical, and historical factors that intervene in the development of machismo, especially in Latin America. This literature mainly discusses aspects such as the system of male superiority, subordination of women, and power conflicts among men. Although the negative or destructive aspects of machismo are recognized, attention is also paid to the positive aspects, among which the authors mention courage, strength, responsibility, perseverance, and protecting the family. De la Cancela (1981) calls this literature "culturalist."

To illustrate how repetitive and uncritical the writings on machismo can be, I will briefly examine two works published in Puerto Rico at the end of the seventies. Working from a very small bibliography and from his observations in the Dominican Republic and other Latin American countries,[6] Mejía Ricart explains that

> among the men of the region [machismo] tends to generate a social role that includes twenty principal characteristics. These fall into two groups of ten; those of the first group are related to male sexual behavior and the others are tied to the position adopted by the individual vis-à-vis society. (1975, 354–358)

The first group includes the following:

1. Sexual potency: proving to himself and others his great sexual potency
2. *Don Juanismo*: tending to possess an unlimited num-

ber of women, virgins if possible, and to support several women simultaneously

3. *Parranderismo*: irrepressibly wanting to go out with male friends to drink alcohol and meet prostitutes or "occasional girlfriends"

4. Masculine exhibitionism: partially or totally exhibiting those parts of the body that characterize the male sex (the penis, chest hair, muscles, etc.), whether emphasizing gestures, tone of voice, manner of walking, or other behaviors that are customary in men

5. Coprolalia: consciously using dirty language and making obscene jokes

6. Cult of virginity: demanding virginity in the woman as a test of her innocence, combined with defending his sisters' or close female relatives' virginity; it is also a source of pride to deflower all those women whom he is able to convince or force

7. Sexual repression of woman: relegating the woman to a merely passive role in the search for her mate; likewise for sexual intercourse

8. Taboo on sexual subjects: both men and women abstaining from commenting to each other about their sexual experiences and desires, with the exception of men with prostitutes and partying girlfriends

9. Fertility: identifying masculinity with the procreation of many children

10. Procreation of male offspring: procreating a large number of males rather than females is a sign of machismo for the man

In the second list there appear:

1. Stereotyping of male superiority: men being superior over women in both physical and intellectual features

2. Emotional rigidity: showing aloofness from loved ones and apparent rigidity in critical situations
3. Generational distancing: psychological distancing between the man and younger generations
4. Independence: desiring independence for the man of the machista culture; this desire is encouraged by parents beginning in childhood, while any hint of autonomous conduct in women is hindered
5. Aggressiveness: being physically or psychologically violent is considered the "successful" way of settling differences with others and is one of the most characteristic traits of machismo
6. Power hunger: wanting to achieve and exercise social control in all its various manifestations
7. Physical strength: having strength is an attribute inherent to masculinity
8. Personal courage: including the ability to face danger, even when unnecessary; many carry this to the point of recklessness, but it is without a doubt the touchstone of the constellation of macho traits
9. Honor: identifying honor, which in this context is a mixture of self-esteem, with the behavior of wife and daughters, rather than with his own; condescending treatment of the weak; and courteous treatment of any woman who is not his wife
10. Extravagance: spending much money before strangers— even at the cost of causing daily financial problems in personal life—with the objective of giving a good impression and showing off financial power

The twenty traits represent virtually all the characteristics of machismo that appeared in the literature on the subject at the time that Mejía Ricart's article was published.

No distinction is made between the so-called negative, pathological, or destructive traits and those considered positive. Mejía Ricart gives the impression that all of the traits are reprehensible and none deserve to be preserved. He recognizes that machismo is manifested in an unequal manner in the class structure, with a lesser incidence in the higher classes because women have more economic independence from their husbands, higher prestige, and more power. For him, the middle classes display the greatest manifestations of machismo. Although machismo also exists in the lower classes, variations appear there because women have more sexual freedom than their counterparts in the other social classes. The explanation of the origins of machismo given by Mejía Ricart is very unsatisfactory. The explanation rests upon such factors as the patriarchy inherited by Latin American societies in Western culture, regional economic conditions, wars of independence, and internal struggles. Mejía Ricart concludes the article with a call to conquer machismo.

Uncritically accepting the description of traits that appear in the literature and not submitting them to analysis leads Mejía Ricart to present us with a stereotyped vision of a Latin American man that, nevertheless, appears as a great truth. The major problem with his study is that it does not go beyond an enumeration of the so-called traits. The study also does not distinguish between ideology and behavior. The traits, which in my opinion are actions, seem not to be connected to the social context in which they are expressed.

If we are to go beyond the conceptual limitations of the literature on machismo, then it is fundamental that a distinction be made between ideology and behavior. The masculine ideology, because it is a social construction that favors the masculine and belittles the feminine, places us men in a universe of categories and symbols of power that we reproduce daily. This ideology forms and guides us in our behavior as men. In class societies, these behaviors are manifested unequally and at the same time are articulated in the position that each person occupies in the social hierarchy. For that reason, although there is one ideology, there are various behaviors; they vary according to the power and privileges that each man possesses. The least powerful men and those in the greatest apparent competition with others to demonstrate their manhood resort to acts of behavior that exaggerate attributes of masculinity. The "machismo traits" that appear in Mejía Ricart's article are acts of behavior that manifest class positions and are survival mechanisms used by the least powerful men in class societies.

To illustrate this last point, let us analyze one of the traits that Mejía Ricart lists: coprolalia. The use of dirty language and obscene jokes is a part of daily life for men and women and is, in addition, completely influenced by class origin. In some specific social encounters, this language is used; in others, its use is prohibited. Although coprolalia is more common among men, not all men use it. Additionally, this language needs to be seen within the social context in which it appears; for example, in peace-filled or conflict-filled situations. This sort of language tends to be more common in situations of conflict, but a man does not need to resort to this language to assert his masculinity. This kind of analysis could be done with each of the traits.

Basically, Mejía Ricart's article repeats the clinical approach by presenting machismo as a quasi sickness and as a compensatory mechanism. In not attempting to transcend the limitations inherent in the term itself, Mejía Ricart cannot explain the complexity of the construction of masculinity and of masculine ideologies. As I have pointed out earlier (Ramírez 1989), representations of machismo, both popular and academic, describe us men as beings who are very homogeneous in our behavior. Nevertheless, our histories, literature, and ethnologies—without denying the powerful presence of colonels and patriarchs—indicate that we resemble Taso more than *charro*.[7]

The uncritical acceptance of machismo also appears in one of the studies in the area of gender and education that was most influential in Puerto Rico during the eighties (Picó 1979). The purpose of this study was to determine the degree of machismo present in elementary education by analyzing the subjects taught and the graphic content of school texts in Spanish and social studies. The definition of machismo given by Isabel Picó reproduces the traditional approach to the term in the literature:

> We take "machismo" to be the set of attitudes, beliefs, and behavior that results from belief in the superiority of one sex over the other. Within this vision of the world, the superior sex is the male. This superiority is due to various aspects: physical, intellectual, characterological, cultural, and sexual. Machismo is expressed essentially through habits, traditions, and attitudes that are discriminatory toward the female sex. It is a cultural phenomenon originating in economic conditions that it transcends in order to become cause and effect, and thus legitimates the inequalities that exist in society. (v)

The researchers designed a questionnaire to identify the stereotyping of sex roles in textbooks through an analysis of the illustrations and content of the texts. Included among the questions were the number of people, their professions, and positions as well as children's games and activities. The analysis found stereotyping even in the stories in which animals appeared. In the stories, there was a higher representation of males than females, and every animal was assigned characteristics traditionally considered to be proper to each sex. The women were presented in numerically smaller proportion than the men and subordinate to them. With respect to the manifestation of emotions in the social sciences texts, feelings and tenderness were expressed by the female figures. In general, the vision of the woman that appeared in the texts was that of a consumer, in charge of buying basic provisions, while the men worked and were the breadwinners; that is, there was a vision of the woman as dependent upon her man to satisfy her basic needs. The article points out the omission of women in the teaching of history. Texts glorify the male figure, and the role of females was either not mentioned or minimized. When a female appeared, it was primarily in the role as wife or mother. Picó concludes: "The social studies texts are characterized by an approach to the history of peoples which ignores women's presence and reduces their importance in virtually all the historical and cultural periods of the peoples studied" (60).

In addition to the analyses of texts, 128 female elementary school teachers were surveyed in the San Juan school district, and teacher-student interaction in the classrooms was observed in order to gauge the degree of stereotyping of sex roles. In analyzing the survey, it was found that teachers were aware of the sex roles assigned to each gender in Puerto Rican society. Most of the teachers favored greater female participation in positions of power and in decision making, as well as the sharing of domestic work and child raising with men. They were more conservative with respect to supporting the traditional concepts of sexuality, especially the importance of preserving a woman's virginity. The observations of teacher-student interaction found differential treatment on the basis of gender in both the number of times that boys and girls were called upon and the reasons for doing so.

The importance of this research is undeniable for demonstrating how male domination is perpetuated in Puerto Rican society by presenting women as subordinate, dependent beings in contrast to the more or less powerful male image. Picó, however, like those who uncritically use the category of "machismo," cannot escape the limitations inherent to the category. The study has three important limitations. First, Picó does not elaborate on the assertion that machismo is a cultural phenomenon. Second, she does not discuss the economic conditions that, according to her, give rise to machismo. Finally, she asserts that machismo is equivalent to sexism.

I disagree with the last assertion for many reasons. Sexism is an ideology that is of great specificity and lacks the contradictions and ambiguities of the term "machismo." Sexism is based on biological differences between men and women and, in turn, maintains that these differences are expressed by or are translated into cultural characteristics or behaviors. Sexism argues a specificity about each sex, an inherent inequality that attributes to one sex superiority over the other. In other words, sexist ideology posits subordination, with the corresponding sexual hierarchy and social asymmetry directed toward undervaluing femaleness. However, the sexist ideology is also applied to sexual orientations that break from total heterosexuality, as in the case of homosexuality and lesbianism. Therefore, it is a sexist position to maintain that specific human populations have greater or less sexual potency or pleasure because of sexuality.

Examples are references to "black men's immense sexual cravings" and the perpetuation of the Latin lover myth, as if all Latin American men were the incarnation of Porfirio Rubirosa.[8]

In contrast to the approaches of the studies summarized above, there is an exception to the literature, a study of machismo with a different orientation. I refer to the doctoral dissertation of Víctor De la Cancela (1981), who makes a distinction between the traditional and culturalist orientations in the literature on machismo. De la Cancela labels as "traditional" those approaches that are inscribed within the clinical discourse and stress machismo as a personality characteristic, and he calls "culturalist" those that take into account sociohistorical factors. This distinction allows him to distance himself from the usual approaches that appear in the literature of machismo and to design his research from a dialectical perspective, which aims to "discover the interactive, interconnected, and contradictory aspects of machismo given a specific socio-historical context" (77). The dialectical perspective that De la Cancela uses is based on a criticism leveled at the dominant Anglo-American culture in the United States. In this culture, Latin cultural manifestations are not generally accepted, and some are considered an aberration. In opposition to this tendency, especially in psychology, De la Cancela emphasizes the importance of understanding the culture from a relativist perspective, as the result of a prevailing social order that is due to historical changes. Specifically, De la Cancela sees the Latin culture in the United States as an adaptation that is due to that population's subordination. Applying this perspective to his analysis of machismo reveals both the marginal position of Latins in the economic and social structures and the consequences of that marginalization. De la Cancela believes that his dialectical approach explains machismo as a phenomenon that is the product of a multiplicity of causes, among which socioeconomical factors prevail.

In an exhaustive empirical study, De la Cancela interviewed twenty Puerto Rican males and twenty Puerto Rican females with identical demographic characteristics of age, place of residence, education, and income. The people interviewed were between 18 and 21, had high school educations or lower, had annual incomes less than $8,000, and lived in the northeastern United States. To gather the data, a questionnaire containing 245 items was used. The questionnaire combined the Likert scale, true-false statements, and open questions; it was divided into five sections: demographic information on the subjects, masculine identity, parenting, male-female relationships, and alienation (understood as the subjects' perception of the degree of control they had in their lives and their interaction with U.S. society). Through statistical analysis of the answers, De la Cancela arrived at four conclusions. The first was that being a man included both positive and negative aspects. In their answers, the women tended to stress negative traits and to associate machismo with sexual issues, while the men emphasized positive aspects and associated the term with responsibilities. The second conclusion had to do with the way in which machismo influences the concept of Puerto Rican paternity. "Being a man" implies that the man is an important figure in the family and is available to help raise his children. His function is not merely disciplinary; it is understood that the father-child relationship should be one of confidence, respect, acceptance, and friendship. The third conclusion is somewhat mixed, stating that Puerto Rican men believe that there are differences between their values and those of the Anglos, in the sense that the Anglos are considered more liberal with and faithful to their women and less interested in having large families. Puerto Ricans also felt that they have less control over their own lives because they have lower incomes and less education. In addition, because of the precariousness of their situation, machismo expresses the ability to be a good worker and the family breadwinner. Finally, De la Cancela concludes that there is a difference between the concept of machismo held by Puerto Ricans and that which prevails in the dominant schools of the social sciences. The Puerto Rican men interviewed did not undervalue women; their relationships with male peers were not particularly charged with tension; and they did not establish a correlation between machismo, war, and revolutions.

In my opinion, despite its efforts and attempts to offer a dialectical interpretation of machismo that integrates contradictory elements or strengths and explains cultural, socioeconomical, and historical factors, this research does not transcend the limitation inherent in the term "machismo."

Despite its limited power of explanation, the use of the term "machismo" to describe male behavior continues in Puerto Rico. In a relatively recent publication on the history of the Barrio Caimito in Río Piedras, Fernando Picó (1989) speaks of how rooted "machista values" are in that community. To illustrate, he lists the following "values":

> the division of the male and female spaces in the house and on the street, the difference in the education given to boys and girls, the double standard in male and female sexual mores, the exaggerated admiration of male behavior, the mystification of maternity, the cult of

weapons and other symbols of virility, taking away the salary that women earn . . . (136)

Trapped by the generalized use of the term, Picó does not notice that he is describing the Barrio Caimito version of gender differences that exist in many human societies. In other research on gender in Puerto Rico, the concept of "sexism" is used (Azize Vargas 1992; Ostolaza Bey 1989). For example, Ostolaza Bey, in spite of her attempts to define sexism, still confuses one term with another when she says: "For ideological analysis, the term 'sexism' replaces the better known and coarser term 'machismo'" (22).

In conclusion, the uncritical reproduction of the terminology of machismo and the use of "machismo" as an analytical category perpetuate an erroneous conceptualization of Latin American men. Although the ethnocentric and class approaches of early studies have been somewhat modified, the reductionist element remains unchanged. Basically, reductionism consists of presenting men as very homogeneous beings and not adequately taking into account the complexity of masculinity and the great variations in its manifestations. Much of the literature on machismo and the writings of some feminists erase the existence of some differences between men and women that, although culturally constructed, serve as a basis for social order and do not necessarily imply inequality. When pre-state communities, organized by kinship systems, established the spheres of gender and human reproduction, they did not necessarily have the intention of establishing a system of inequality. They were recognizing and affirming differences and designing some controls assigned to each person in the cultural system; this is what Illich (1982) calls the vernacular gender.[9] Another great limitation of the literature on machismo is placing too much emphasis on behaviors and not paying enough attention to the discourses. As we shall see later on, in our discourses, we Latin American men present, defend, and justify our hegemonic position, and in the study of the discourses, we find the elements that form our masculinity in all of its heterogeneity, contradictions, and anxieties.

2

The

Construction

of

Masculinity

It happens that I become tired of being a man.

—Pablo Neruda

Pointing out the conceptual limitations of studies on machismo and their limited explanatory power, in addition to my concern about the permanence of the category of machismo and the widespread use of the term "machismo" to describe and explain Puerto Rican men, should not be taken to be a justification of male domination and of men's privileges. On the contrary, I maintain that the uncritical reproduction of that category is a pitfall with respect to understanding the construction of masculinity, the relationships between genders, and the possibility of changing the parameters of masculinity. In contrast to the theoretical deficiencies of the literature on machismo, more recent studies on sexuality, masculine ideologies, and the construction of masculinity offer better explanations of how we become, or are made into, men. Theoretical approaches help to understand the complexity of the cultural construction of genders (MacCormack and Strathern 1980; Ortner and Whitehead 1981); the uses of sexuality (Dover 1978; Herdt 1981; Keuls 1985); relationships between genders (Reiter 1975; Sanday 1981); and relationships between men (Brandes 1980; Herdt 1982; Herzfeld 1985).

Masculine ideologies are cognitive and discursive constructions that prevail in societies structured on the basis of asymmetrical relationships between genders. These constructions are articulated in shows of strength and games of power that display a multiplicity of manifestations—a product of the human species' cultural plurality. In complex societies, these constructions are expressed in differentiated and contradictory forms. Tackling the subject of ideology is no easy task; in this century, ideology is one of the major subjects of debate in the social sciences, especially among Marxist schools of thought. The discussion of those debates lies outside the scope and objectives of this book, although I think it necessary to point out that I use the concept of ideology in two senses: as a mode of perceiving and interpreting experiences and as a mode to influence actions. From an anthropological perspective, the concept of ideology is not limited to political direction and action but is considered an integral part of the social, economic, and supernatural spheres (Nash 1979). I am not of the opinion that ideology is exclusively or primarily *false* awareness or *false* representation; rather, I take ideology to be both the system of beliefs characteristic of a class or group and the general process of the production of ideas and meanings (Williams 1977).

In the discussion of masculinity that follows, I shall use the plural to avoid falling into reductionism. Although there are many common elements, I do not agree with the view that there exists a uniform and static masculinity, which is shared equally by all men across time and space. To understand that which we call "masculinity," we should approach this study from the perspective of the human species' cultural diversity. Sex is a biological differentiation of the species associated with reproduction, while gender is a construction of the species in a cultural medium. Given the abundant ethnographic evidence of this cultural diversity, it is clear that we will find not a single ideology but rather masculine ideologies, plural, which are the product of, and simultaneously due to, diversity. Since cultures are not static but rather undergo constant change, within society masculinity is subject to modifications through time. As Brittan states:

> In talking about the masculine ideology, we are therefore not only referring to the economic and political position of men, but also how they define and theorize sexuality and gender. And it is the variability of these theories and definitions that, to a large extent, constitute the historical specificity of this or that form of masculinity. (1989, 18)

Every society differentiates between genders, specifies the spheres of masculinity and femininity, and assigns to each gender specific attributes, characteristics, and expectations. People are recognized and evaluated on the basis of the way they fulfill the demands assigned to them. Culture offers cues and instructions so that people may make their own gender identity, in order to evaluate and esteem themselves as the incarnation and representation of their gender.

Therefore, masculinity and femininity are not a reality separate from the individual; they are a cultural construction whose basis is not biological—even though the cultural construction is based on biological differences—but constructed, designed, agreed to, and upheld by a system of beliefs, attributes, and expectations. With respect to this point, Whitehead says:

> When I speak of cultural constructions of gender, I simply mean the ideas that give social meaning to physical differences between the sexes, rendering two biological classes, male and female, into two social classes, men and women, and making the social relationships in which men and women stand toward each other appear reasonable and appropriate. (1981, 83)

The constructionist approach maintains that the categories through which we perceive, evaluate, and think are socially constructed. They do not exist independently of the individual; they do not constitute a reality that we approach in order to know objectively. The categories are social constructions with cultural specificity. This point of view emphasizes the active dimension of individuals who, employing the guidelines that their culture lays down, construct their reality in accordance with or in opposition to these guidelines. In anthropology this process is generally referred to as "cultural construction," while other disciplines call it "social construction" (Stein 1992). The artificiality of cultural institutions, taken as being juxtaposed against nature, as well as their construction, variability, and relativity, is an old topic in anthropology, found even as early as the pioneering and controversial works of Benedict (1946) and Mead (1950). The current constructionism is characterized by the systematic identification of the "cultural and social processes to which culturally variable sex and gender notions might be related" (Ortner and Whitehead 1981, 1). As Jorge-Rivera points out in his use of gender and sexuality studies, the constructionist approach

> states that gender behavior—and all sexual manifestation—is influenced by the set of historical-social norms, ideas, symbols, and meanings which are in turn constituted *in, for and by* the individual. (1989, 4)

The influence of the constructionist approach in gender and sexual orientation studies, and the beginning of the modern debate on this approach,[1] can be traced to the influence of the work of McIntosh (1992) and Foucault (1990a).[2]

McIntosh begins her analysis by first positing that homosexuality is usually conceived as a condition characterizing certain individuals and that many people assume that there are two types of people: homosexuals and heterosexuals. She points out that Bieber (1965) and other authors present a third type, the bisexual, when they discover that it is not possible to dichotomize sexual orientation because there are people who have relations with both sexes. McIntosh criticizes this position, and, using the sociological concept of stigmatization, she suggests that from a medical or psychiatric perspective, the idea of homosexuality as a condition operates as a mechanism of social control. To say that homosexuality is a social problem is to condemn some people and stigmatize them as deviants. On the contrary, McIntosh proposes that the homosexual be seen as acting out a role, which is defined in terms of expectations. Using historical and ethnographic evidence, she stresses that such a role exists in some societies but not in others, in which sexual intercourse with the same sex is accepted as an integral part of the variety of sexual patterns. In other words, evidence shows that preference for the same sex can occur without creating the category of "homosexual," which allegedly was invented by Dr. Karoly Maria Benkert in Germany in 1869 (Posner 1992, 125; Pronger 1990, 87). In those societies that do not have the category of "homosexual," sexual expression with the same sex is not considered separately from sexuality in general, and those who practice it are not "labeled." This practice was the case during Athens's classical period, when adult citizens and married men had sexual and amorous relationships with youths in a complex, institutionalized, and highly ritualized form of homoeroticism. By using the ancient Athenians as an example, I am not trying to give the impression that homoeroticism is an archaic or bizarre practice. Homoeroticism is both an ancient and modern practice. In several societies, among them ours, homoeroticism is most visible in situations in which men do not have access to women, such as in our prison system. Some authors, such as Richard Posner (1992), label as "opportunistic homosexuality" same-sex relations that are not "mediatized" by the category "homosexual." As this topic is discussed at length in another part of this book, it should suffice to refer to a sexual identity study in Costa Rica in which the authors have recognized men who have sex with other men without being incarcerated or isolated from women yet who identify themselves as lovers of women and do not consider themselves homosexuals.

> It is they whom we have in mind when we say that a lance [sic] may be a male, that a *querida* may be a *querido*. If one were to ask them to what extent they love men, they might have to pause to consider their reply (assuming they were willing to search themselves for an honest answer), because the question would not

have occurred to them. Their relatively rare sex with men is not important enough to affect their self-identity. (Kutsche and Page 1992, 11)

Foucault (1990a) believes that sexualities are constantly made and modified and discusses the rise of the modern idea of sexuality in the West and the way sexuality is constructed in a specific social and historical context. He differentiates between carnal, sensory, and sexual experiences. Sexual experiences are taken to be the product of a system of knowledge and modes of power. According to Foucault, modern Western sexuality is characterized by an explosion of discourses of power and knowledge in which sexual meanings and doctrines are constantly generated in a culture obsessed with sexuality.

> The society that emerged in the nineteenth century—bourgeois, capitalist, or industrial society, call it what you will—did not confront sex with a fundamental refusal of recognition. On the contrary, it put into operation an entire machinery for producing true discourses concerning it. Not only did it speak of sex and compel everyone to do so; it also set out to formulate the uniform truth of sex. As if it suspected sex of harboring a fundamental secret. As if it needed this production of truth. As if it was essential that sex be inscribed not only in an economy of pleasure but in an ordered system of knowledge. (69)

Another important contribution in the development of the constructionist approach can be found in the anthology edited by Ortner and Whitehead (1981). In the introduction, the authors indicate that the articles in the collection are characterized by their approach to studies on gender, sexuality, and reproduction; these phenomena are treated as symbols to which every society attributes specific meanings. Each symbol can be understood by placing it and studying it within the context of the entire symbology of each society. Therefore, the articulation between symbols and meanings becomes the object of study.

Masculine ideologies are cultural constructions that create asymmetrical relationships between genders. The asymmetry consists of making distinctions in such a way that the tasks and functions assigned to each person, as with other attributes such as prestige or power, are neither proportional nor comparable. The levels of asymmetry vary from one society to another, from the strictest separation and inequality between genders to systems in which women enjoy certain rights and have a relative "equality" with men, as happens in some modern democracies. Asymmetrical relationships are created on the basis of superiority of men and the subordination, devaluation, and inferiorizing of women. Simultaneously, the sphere of masculinity is valued, praised, and privileged. The origins of this system, built by and for men, in which women are the object of what Ostolaza Bey (1989) rightly calls "the sex-gender system with masculine dominance," have occupied a prominent place in the literature of anthropology since the early seventies, especially in the works of feminist anthropologists. The system is built upon the basis of inequality. The nature, origins, and evolution of that inequality are points of debate in modern anthropology and are linked both to changing ideas about woman's role in the evolution of societies and to recent interpretations of hunting and gathering societies.[3]

In societies having dominant masculine ideologies, we men are constantly constructing ourselves, and at times, as

Neruda says, we become tired. What does it mean when we say that being men means constantly making ourselves? Why do we become tired? What goes into being a man? What does "masculinity" mean? How is masculinity constructed? To answer these questions, I will examine several anthropological studies that analyze the sphere of masculinity in many societies.

Gilmore (1990) approaches the study of the elements of masculinity—what it means to be a man—from an ethnographic and comparative perspective. For this purpose, he analyzes masculine ideologies in several societies selected by a cultural sampling. This technique allows him to obtain representation both of different types of social formations, from the simplest to the most complex, and of different geographic or cultural areas. The societies in the sample include rural communities in the Mediterranean; Truk Island in Micronesia; the Mehinaku Indians of the Xingú forest reserve in central Brazil; the Samburu of northern Kenya; the Sambia of the New Guinea highlands, China, India, Japan, and Tahiti; and the Semai of central Malaysia. Except for the Sambia of Tahiti and the Semai, he finds a common element, a dominant tendency in the construction of masculinity: to be a man is more than the mere fact of having been born male. The man has to demonstrate his manhood and have his manhood recognized. Gilmore says:

> Amongst most of the peoples that anthropologists are familiar with, true manhood is a precious and elusive status beyond mere maleness, a hortatory image that men and boys aspire to and that their culture demands of them as a measure of belonging. . . . A restricted status, there are always men who fail the test. These are the negative examples, the effete men, the men-who-

are-no-men, held up scornfully to inspire conformity to the glorious ideal. (17)

Gilmore's main argument is that masculine ideologies make an indispensable contribution to the continuity of social systems and to the psychological integration of men into their community (3). In most of the societies Gilmore analyzed, masculinity was tied to the requirement that the man be a provider. Being a provider does not mean that the woman's contribution to the sustenance and well-being of the domestic unit and to the community in general is denied; the emphasis lies on the recurrence of three notions of masculinity: first, the association of masculinity with emphasis on hard work and effective enterprise; second, the relationship between masculinity and bigness, defined not only in physical terms but also in achievements and possessions, and consequently the association of wealth with privilege and power; and third, masculinity as a sense of personal accomplishment achieved by positive or authoritative actions that contribute to, or are considered to contribute to, society in general (110). In an overwhelming number of the societies Gilmore studied, masculine ideologies are dominant. Men are assigned the most difficult and dangerous tasks, such as finding "animal protein, fending off predators, and fighting wars" (120). There is ample evidence that supports this conclusion. Gilmore attributes the assignment of the most dangerous tasks to men for two main reasons. The first is that men possess greater upper body strength; the second involves men's contribution to the biological reproduction of the human species: we men are unnecessary after impregnating the woman. In contrast, gestation, birth, and lactation—female functions—are indispensable for the reproduction of the human baby. Gilmore bases his argument on the ideas of Friedl, who points out that for biological reasons, "a population can survive the loss of men more easily than that of women" (1975, 135). Because men are more dispensable, they are assigned tasks of greater risk than those assigned to women, and to confront these risks it is necessary to have a socialization process that trains men to face dangers and not run from them.

> I do not wish to suggest that women have it easier than men, but that their performances are judged by different standards and that these inspire different gender ideals. The main difference seems to be that men are expected to seek out and confront danger as a means of showing valor, while women are more expected to avoid such situations. (Gilmore 1990, 122)

Unlike societies in which masculine ideologies dominate, Gilmore presents the cases of Tahiti and the Semai, which lack masculine ideologies. "The Tahitians and the Semai simply do not seem to care much about manhood" (217). Why? How can that be explained? Admitting that there is insufficient information on these societies to arrive at definite conclusions, Gilmore attributes the absence of a masculine ideology to the fact that in these two societies there are abundant natural resources for survival. They do not hunt, and the economy is cooperative. Therefore, it is unnecessary to assign high-risk tasks to men.[4]

Another matter to be considered in any discussion of the construction of masculinity is sexuality—a fundamental part of masculine ideologies—in its articulation between power and pleasure. However, expressions of sexuality, including its biosocial dimension, vary greatly in human societies, thus making it difficult to generalize.[5] Understanding the nexus between sexuality, power, and masculinity requires us to refer to specific material, to the study of specific societies. Godelier's study (1986) on the Baruya people of New Guinea is an example of the kind of research that allows us to understand these relationships. This study illustrates the connection between sexuality and competition in the construction of masculinity within a classless society. Turning to the study of other societies to understand aspects of our humanity is part of an anthropological tradition based upon the principle that anthropology, as Kluckhohn has said (1957), is a mirror of sorts for human beings because a knowledge of other societies helps us understand ourselves. Godelier analyzes the role of sexuality in the thinking of the men of the Baruya society and shows that each aspect of male domination can be explained on the basis of sexuality. The analysis is focused on three topics: the machinery of male domination, the production of great men, and the ideological justification of this social order (xii).

The Baruya people are found in the Eastern Highlands province of New Guinea. This area was the last to come under Australian colonial administration; the people's first contact with white men was in 1951. Between 1967 and 1979, Godelier studied the Baruya during many periods of fieldwork. In 1979, the society numbered 2,179 individuals scattered in 17 villages located between two valleys at an elevation that varied from 1,610 to 2,300 meters above sea level (1). The social organization consisted of an acephalous tribe of 15 clans divided into lineages, which are also segmented.[6] The kinship system was patrilineal, so that at birth each baby was assigned to the father's lineage or clan. Residence was patrilocal; boys lived near their parents. The marriage system distinguished five kinds of possible unions, but the first of them, called *ginamare*, was considered the norm. This first type of marriage was a system of direct exchange of women between two lineages or segments of a lineage. Of the five types of matrimonial unions, two were infrequent. One of them was when a young boy, who did not have a sister or female cousin to exchange, would approach a couple with a marriageable daughter and by working for them would persuade them to accept him as a son-in-law. The other case was done only with outside members of other tribes, to establish exchange relations using the system of paying for a wife with goods or property. The remaining three systems were based on variations of the system of *ginamare* and eventually reestablished the system of sister exchange. According to Godelier, the system's logic is based on the principle that the only way "one can really compensate the gift of a woman is by giving another woman in exchange" (23) and the fact that the Baruya established that the lineages that offered women were superior to those that received the women. To reestablish the balance of power between lineages, it was necessary to have an exchange mechanism that allowed those that received women to become the offerers.

The economic system of the Baruya was based on horticulture using the slash-and-burn technique. Crops consisted primarily of sweet potato and a by-product of taro for ceremonial uses. Tuber crops were supplemented with pigs bred for food and the production of salt, an important article for exchange. Hunting and gathering had little importance.

The Baruya established a strict division of labor, with specific tasks assigned to each gender in a system in which men were the owners of the land for planting and hunting and, of course, land rights were transferred to men exclusively. Women were excluded from land possession and from making and owning tools. Men lent women tools so that they could do their assigned tasks. Women were also excluded from owning weapons, since hunting and war were tasks reserved for men (12). Making a gender comparison, Godelier finds that the tasks assigned to women have the following characteristics:

a. require less physical strength, or to be more precise, do not entail a great deal of physical effort in a short space of time (as does felling a tree);
b. involve fewer risks of accident (many men are killed climbing the trees to pollard them, gather their fruit, or winkle out opossums, the principal game);
c. require less mutual help or cooperation among individuals—the women work alone much more than the men, carrying out generally more monotonous routine tasks (gathering sweet potatoes, feeding the pigs, cooking, gathering deadwood). (14)

We find again what Gilmore pointed out: tasks that require more physical strength and are of greater risk are assigned to men. But, according to Godelier, male domination does not stem from the social division of labor. On the contrary, Godelier stresses that the social division of labor among the Baruya *presupposes* male domination (14). What makes up this system of domination? How is male superiority over women established, and how is it articulated with sexuality?

The system of male domination is based on six principles for excluding women: (a) women cannot own land but can use it; (b) women cannot own or use the more efficient tools that men use to clean the forest; (c) women cannot own or use weapons; (d) women neither participate in salt production nor exchange goods with other tribes; it is up to the men to obtain the salt bars, which can be used to obtain other goods; (e) women cannot own sacred objects; (f) women occupy a subordinate position in the production of kinship relations because men exchange women through the *ginamare* matrimonial system (29). As a result of the list above, women are subordinate to men in the material, political, and symbolic spheres.

The reproduction and legitimization of the system of male domination are illustrated in the process of turning a boy into a man. As in other societies that consider males superior, men are not born, they are made. The Baruya invest great time and effort in transforming their boys into men through initiation rituals. Godelier indicates that the process includes ten years of sexual segregation. When the time comes to begin the initiation process, boys are separated from their mothers and taken to the men's house, a place where women are not permitted, and are completely isolated from any contact with women. The purpose of the various ceremonies celebrated during that period is to separate the boy from his mother, disconnect him from the world of women, turn him into a man, and prepare him to face women again when he marries. The process is a complete immersion into the world of men through which a boy's masculinity is constructed. The initiation rituals, responsibilities, attributes, and distinctions of masculinity that are gradually revealed to the initiates form a body of privileged knowledge about and for men. It is a secret knowledge that is never shared with women. In contrast, the process of turning a female adolescent into a married women takes less than two weeks and is relatively simple, which makes Godelier question whether it can be considered a true initiation ritual.

Godelier explains the uses of sexuality to support male domination among the Baruya by analyzing how they conceptualize the human reproduction process and the meaning of bodily secretions. For these men, the baby is made from semen. When the semen unites with the mother's vaginal fluids, the sex of the fetus will be determined by the secretion that turns out to be dominant. If the semen prevails, the baby will be a boy. Also, during pregnancy, coitus continues to feed the baby. The natural or biological father creates the body, and the supernatural father, the sun, makes the eyes, nose, mouth, fingers, and toes (51). Semen is life and strength, and for this reason, couples practice oral sex, through which women swallow semen when they need physical strength. The first sexual relation of newlyweds is of this type because semen is considered essential for the production of maternal milk. During the initiation process, young boys swallow semen for many years.[7] This very secret practice is carried out in the men's house because the young boys need semen to "make them grow taller and stronger than women, superior to them, capable of dominating and managing them" (52). Not just any man can give semen to the initiates. Married men cannot do so, because it is considered aggression against young boys for a married man, who uses his penis with women, to place it in an initiate's mouth. Doing so would contaminate the boy, who is in the process of separation from the world of women. Therefore, young unmarried men who have been initiated are the ones who provide semen to the initiates, and they cannot refuse to perform this homoerotic act because it is a fundamental part in this society's construction of masculinity. The practice stops as soon as the man marries. The Baruya believe that the female genitals, their secretions, and, above all, menstrual blood are contaminants, and therefore married men cannot provide semen to initiates. Godelier summarizes their attitude:

The attitude of the men toward menstrual blood, whenever they talk or think about it, verges on hysteria, mingling disgust, repulsion, and, above all, fear. For them, menstrual blood is dirty, and they rank it with those other polluting, repugnant substances, urine and feces. Above all, though, it is a substance that weakens women whenever it flows from them, and it would destroy men's strength if ever it came into contact with their bodies. (58)

Clearly, all of the conceptualization about both the nature and power of bodily secretions and how menstrual blood threatens virility is associated with a series of practices in gender relationships, in rituals of evasion and purification, and in sexual practices in keeping with the belief system.

Godelier maintains that although from the outside the belief system related to menstruation appears to be in negative opposition to the belief system related to semen, it actually is not. On the contrary, menstrual blood forms "a double reality that also contains a positive element" (63), for menstruation is a manifestation of woman's power— "power in the woman's belly" (64). Analyzing the myths in greater depth, Godelier finds that there were periods when women had powers, but they were periods of disorder. According to the myths, order is established when men have control of all the powers. By taking powers from women, a belief system is built to discredit and minimize the importance of women's power, which is expressed in the beliefs about and practices of sexuality. In conclusion, we may say that the Baruya use sexuality "to serve as sign and meaning for things that in fact bear no relation to it" (xii).

The construction of masculinity among the Baruya, the constant process of making men, does not end when one acquires the status of a married man. Among the men themselves, a system of inequality exists. Although the Baruya is not a class society, not all men are equal. Besides their relationships with women, two hierarchical systems that confer power and privilege exist among the men. The first is hereditary and consists of belonging to the lineages that possess sacred objects and magical and religious formulas used in the initiation rituals. This is a system of association. The other system allows individuals to show their abilities through hunting, war, and shamanism; it is a competitive system through which men can acquire more power. Sexuality, competition, and power are elements that constitute the masculine ideologies, not only among the Baruya but in all the societies through time and space in which we men have imposed our hegemony.

3

We the

Boricuas

This town's not big enough for the two of us.[1]

After analyzing the literature on machismo, discussing the construction of masculinity from an anthropological perspective, and showing the concept of social construction as it applies to gender, it is now time to address the main topic of this book: masculinity in Puerto Rico. There are many difficulties to be faced when undertaking this task: (a) the lack of studies on the subject; (b) the presence of previous studies done during the fifties and sixties, in which "masculinity" was treated as "machismo" or as one aspect of studies of domestic groups and the socialization of boys and girls in working-class populations, rural communities (Landy 1965; Wolf 1952), and poor families (Lewis 1966c); (c) the virtual nonexistence of studies of the upper classes; and (d) the profound changes that Puerto Rican society has undergone in the last forty years (Rivera Medina and Ramírez 1985). We are talking about a complex society of approximately six million inhabitants; a society of various basically urban classes, part of whose population lives in U.S. communities and therefore has considerably different experiences than the experiences of those of us raised in Puerto Rico; and emigrants who return with different experiences. We are talking about women who joined the workforce many decades ago, who fight for their rights, and who challenge authority and traditional male domination; about feminist movements that question and fight against the powers and privileges of masculinity, in both public and domestic environments. Clearly, any approach that analyzes masculinity in Puerto Rico needs to consider these factors, variables, and conditions.

The temptation to not write about this subject until doing field research was enormous. I felt, however, that new studies should be due to innovative conceptualizations; arguments should now be made that go beyond denunciation and avoid the repetition of obsolete approaches and paradigms that contribute little to understanding how masculinity is constructed. Following the conceptual frameworks that were presented in the introduction, my intention is to embark on a reflection of the construction of masculinity in Puerto Rico: to delve into *how* we become men (starting from the elements that we share, such as sexuality, its materialization in the genitals, and power) and into the privileges and hardships associated with our masculinity (Rivera Medina 1991).

Sexuality

In Puerto Rico, as in other societies, the masculine ideology stresses sexuality. The male is an essentially sexual being, or at least he should look and act like one. He should enjoy his sexuality, declare it, boast about it, feel proud of it, and, above all, show it. The macho takes delight in women and—sometimes in a vulgar way—reproduces on a daily basis what the great Puerto Rican bard Palés Matos expresses in a poem:

Culipandeando la Reina avanza
y de su inmensa grupa resbalan
meneos cachondos que el gongo cuaja
en ríos de azúcar y de melaza.
Prieto trapiche de sensual zafra,
el caderamen, masa con masa,
exprime ritmos, suda que sangra,
y la molienda culmina en danza.

Swinging her behind, the Queen makes her advance
And from her large backside rolls down an avalanche
Of sexy shimmy moves that rhythms beat down
Into rivers of molasses and sugar—sweet and brown
Black sugarmill of sensuous cane crop
Baby-making hips and booty mounds don't stop
Squeezing out the rhythms—a blood and sweat trance
Until all the grinding culminates in dance. (1964, 233)

Women are objects of pleasure, so long as men abide by the taboo of incest and give the respect that is expected toward those women who are part of the family.[2] This idea applies especially to the "other woman" or one who still has not been conquered. The woman is for pleasure, penetration, possession, *para comérsela* (to be eaten).[3] The macho seduces, conquers, and takes, and uses his sexual power in keeping with an old saying: *Yo suelto mi gallo, los demás que recogan sus gallinas* (I'm letting my cock loose, you'd better hide your hens). The macho pleases and satisfies his "hens." He pursues, punishes, repudiates, or devalues those women who reject him or pay no attention to his demands. Some men beat and sometimes even kill this last type of woman. Sexual harassment and violence against women are evidence of this orientation toward conquest and the use of sexuality in its aggressive articulation of power with pleasure.[4]

Conquest is not undertaken indiscriminately. Each man has his own particular standards of what an attractive woman is. There may be a few women or many who do not interest him, but when the man finds what he considers to be *una buena hembra* (a good-looking woman) or, as teenagers say, *un tronco de mami* (a babe), a macho sees it as his duty to go for the conquest. This process is also influenced by class and color differences and the relative power or influence that a man might have or believe he can have over a woman, or the relative equality that allows him to make the initial move. As in all societies with classes, in which the women of the highest class are "reserved" for the men of their class, a Puerto Rican man does not try to seduce or conquer a woman who is socially or economically superior to him, unless the encounter occurs in a neutral environment, where class, power, or privilege differences are not involved or are minimized, or unless she sends signals that she is willing. With the exception of situations of sexual harassment, women are not passive or unselfish in this game of sexuality. They participate if they think the man is attractive, whether physically or for reasons such as wealth and power. Wealth and power do not imply that Puerto Rican women believe in the saying *el hombre, al igual que el oso, mientras más feo más hermoso* (the man, just like the bear, the uglier he is, the handsomer), similar to the "cavemantype" attraction.

The aim of male sexuality is penetration, and sexual

activity culminates in orgasm and ejaculation. If these two acts do not occur, the Puerto Rican man feels that the sexual act is not completed. In Puerto Rico, penetration may be oral, anal, or vaginal, but vaginal seems to be the preference.[5] Oral penetration is mainly part of foreplay to increase excitement, and not all women are willing to take part in oral sex. Foreplay seeks to increase pleasure before penetration, to further eroticize the encounters; however, foreplay does not completely satisfy the man. Although common, masturbation is considered a substitute activity for "real" sex, coitus, and is performed when no partner is available or the situation does not allow penetration. Masturbation does not offer the same pleasure as penetration, and Puerto Ricans call it *un resuelve* (a solution). Both penetration and ejaculation require that the man maintain an erection. Given that complex physiological, psychological, and erotic factors intervene in maintaining the erection and achieving orgasm, the man should be focused and in complete control of the situation. This creates much anxiety, and for the reasons listed above, the control over the sexual act that the man has or tries to have is geared toward maintaining the erection, reaching orgasm, satisfying himself, and finally, satisfying the woman. With respect to penile erection, Masters and Johnson say the following:

> The human male's first ... response to ... sexual stimulation is penile erection. There may be only a minimum degree of sexual tension present before this response pattern has been completed. After full penile erection has been attained, the excitement phase may extend for the briefest of intervals or for a matter of many minutes in direct parallel to the intensity of or variation in any form of successful sexual stimulation.

Psychosensory diversion has been created frequently in the laboratory during excitement-phase response. Penile erection may be impaired easily by the introduction of asexual stimuli, even though sexual stimulation is continued simultaneously. Despite constantly maintained somatogenic penile stimulation, a sudden loud noise, vocalization on an extraneous subject, or an obvious change in lighting, temperature, or attendant personnel may result in partial or even complete loss of penile erection. (1966, 182–183)

Satisfying a woman or believing that he has satisfied her is very important for the man. The need to bring her to orgasm or many orgasms, in addition to giving her pleasure, is due to the male's presentation as a powerful individual. In addition, this need is in keeping with the belief that a sexually unsatisfied woman is a potential adulteress because she may find, or look for, another man *que se lo haga mejor* (who will do it better for her). I know of cases in which men who have occasional female sex partners whom they consider to be especially hot masturbate before the encounter in order to lengthen the time it takes them to achieve another orgasm. Of course they would never tell the women they did this. In turn, there are men who are so sure of their control over their women or are so insensitive to them that they do not worry about their partner's satisfaction, and they are only interested in their own pleasure.

Sexuality and Power

In Puerto Rico, as in all of Latin America and the Mediterranean, the masculine ideology is embodied in the genitals and is articulated with sexuality and power. In the case of Andalusia, Brandes says the following:

An important component of the masculine self-image
[is revealed] throughout Andalusia: the locus of power
and will, of emotions and strength, lies within the male
genitals. Men speak as if they are impelled to act according to opinions and desires that originate in their
testicles or penis. (1981, 230–231)

Pitt-Rivers (1966, 1977) says the same for the Mediterranean area. In Sicily, according to Blok, a "real man" is "a
man with big testicles" (1981, 432–433); Campbell (1966)
arrives at the same conclusion about the Sarkatsani of
Greece.

Phallocentrism, a cultural code in which the erect phallus or penis symbolizes power, and its articulation with pleasure are archaic (Thorn 1990). According to Vanggaard (1972),
phalluses carved in stone in Greece are very old, and during
the archaic and classical periods, phallic cults were very
prominent in the religious system. These cults also flour-
ished during the Roman Empire and in societies in northern Europe. In an excellent analysis of sexual politics in
Athens from the classical era until the end of the Periclean
era (A.D. 430), Keuls discusses the importance of phallic cults
and the entire power system generated in what she calls a
"phallocracy": "a combination of male supremacy and the
cult of power and violence" (1985, 13). The phallus became
the symbol of male power, which was constantly reaffirmed.
"Athenian men habitually displayed their genitals, and their
city was studded with statues of gods with phalluses hap-
pily erect" (2).

Although the ancient phallic cults were eradicated by
Christianity (Vanggaard 1972), phallic symbolism has not
disappeared from male mentalities. Today that symbolism
is still found in many societies, and in North and South

America the symbolism appears in discourses of the "fuckers" and "fuckees": the meanings that Mexicans give to *el chingón* and *el chingado*; the distinction that Puerto Ricans make between *el que clave* and *el clavado*; and in all the constructions the Americans make between the two terms.

In his famous, classic essay (1961) about the essence of "Mexican-ness," Octavio Paz discusses all the meanings of the verb *chingar* (to fuck) and its derivatives. He says that in most places in Central and South America, the word is associated with alcoholic beverages and also with the idea of failure.

> Almost everywhere, *chingarse* means to be made a fool of, to be involved in a fiasco. In some parts of South America, *chingar* means to molest, to censure, to ridicule. It is always an aggressive verb. (76)

As I have previously noted, the verb and its derivatives have many meanings in Mexico. Paz adds, "It is a magical word: a change of tone, a change of inflection is enough to change its meaning" (76). When Mexicans want to acclaim their "Mexican-ness," they shout *¡Viva México, hijos de la Chingada!* (Long live Mexico, you motherfuckers), a yell of affirmation that "we shout . . . on the fifteenth of September, the anniversary of independence" (75). The verb also denotes violence, "an emergence from oneself to penetrate another by force" (76). *Chingar* is to destroy, break, rip open; therefore Paz concludes that "*Chingar*, then, is to do violence to another. The verb is masculine, active, cruel: it stings, wounds, gashes, and stains. And it provokes a bitter, resentful satisfaction" (77).

In Puerto Rico, *chingar* is synonymous with "fornicate." The verb has no other uses or meanings, and a *chingón* is an individual who has a lot of sex. The Puerto Rican equivalent of the Mexican *el chingar* is *el clavar*. The Puerto Rican male *clava* and is careful, but not always successful, to not get *clava'o*. The word comes from *clavo* (nail), which is forcibly inserted into a wall or object. *Clavar* means to "penetrate" and denotes violence, domination, and power. During the student protests and strikes of the seventies and eighties at the Río Piedras Campus of the University of Puerto Rico, groups of strikers mobilized around the campus asking students and professors who were in the classrooms to join the protest. When they did not agree to join, the demonstrators closed the doors and nailed them shut so that those who were not supportive were not able to leave the rooms. Then they would tell the story of this male professor and that female professor and who had nailed them in the room, and the story would spread around campus. The remarks generated laughter from the demonstrators, who gave a double meaning to the expression, showing both force and sexual penetration.

When a Puerto Rican loses a fight, is hurt, or is harmed, he says, *me clavaron* (they fucked me). To describe a person who is dominated, subjugated, or subordinated, they say *lo tienen clava'o* (he's whipped). This is mostly male talk used among people who are trusted, and, of course, it is not heard in the public sphere. Since *clavar* also means sexual penetration, we men, swollen with pride and pleasure when referring to sex, say *le di tremenda clavada* (boy, did I nail her). Intonation and body language reinforce the meaning of power that one wishes to convey. *Clavar* not only becomes a reaffirmation of masculinity itself but also takes away masculinity from someone else and reduces, devalues, and denigrates a man, placing him in the sphere of the feminine and making him equal to a penetrated woman.[6]

The discourses of Boricuas are equally charged with symbolism in that the penis and the testicles are highly valued, while the female genitals, the anus, and the buttocks—objects of pleasure—are devalued.[7] The genitals become the male power center. Puerto Rican men commonly touch, scratch, and stroke their genitals in public, although the act is influenced by class origin and their position in society. Men from middle and high classes are more cautious and control themselves much more to not touch their genitals in public. This does not necessarily mean that they are less influenced by the mechanisms of power that emanate from the male genitals. With regard to this idea, Rodríguez Juliá comments on a boy's photograph:

> They have dressed him as his dad dresses, since he has to begin assuming the father's testicular obsession; the mom, between feeling pleased and uncomfortable, hits his hand so he does not touch his wee-wee so much, but the little boy knows very well the import of that real or imagined inconvenience at the fork of his pants on his manly beliefs and moves them into place, since they are so big that they do not fit in his underwear. Maybe soon that bad habit will disappear; but getting up from a chair, propping your feet against the wall, enjoying a joke every Friday on the corner, going into the batter's box, are actions that were inevitably accompanied with the gesture of putting your hand on your balls. (1988, 82)

The habit has not disappeared and is common among the working class and the traditional sectors. Quite often, these men are seen in front of a bar, big or small, with a beer or a drink in one hand while the other grabs the genitals. It

seems that the less power and control there is in other factors of men's existence, the more emphasis on their genitals as a center of power.

In their discourses, Puerto Rican men say that a person
who has power, courage, and strength has *cojones* (balls); a
person who does not have these factors is less manly, a
pendejo (jerk). An explicit act of power is called *pasarse por
los huevos* or *pasarse por los cojones* (to be in control). A
man who is *encojonado* (pissed off) is a man who is offended,
bothered, and furious to reassert himself in what he values—his manliness, in that his emotions are connected to
his genitals.[8] All Puerto Rican men, regardless of our social
origin or position in society, use this language to a greater
or lesser degree. Its use increases in situations of conflict,
when there is a great deal of tension, and when our power—
our masculinity—is challenged. The language has been built
by and for men. The language is used in confrontation between men. Although sometimes it is directed toward
women, it is mostly directed toward other men. The most
common insults heard among men in the street and on the
highways of Puerto Rico are *pendejo* (jerk), *cabrón* (asshole
or son of a bitch), *maricón* (fag), *mamabicho* and *huelebicho*
(cocksucker), words all aimed at emphasizing the lack of
manliness in another person. This language is also used in
situations in which there is trust.

In a book based on the life of former governor Luis
Muñoz Marín, the author, Enrique Bird Piñero (1991), al-
ludes to two occasions on which one of the participants
makes reference to Luis Muñoz Rivera—father of Muñoz
Marín and an outstanding politician at the end of the last
century and into the present one—as an individual with
balls. In the first situation, when the author was a teenager,
he asked his uncle by marriage, Antonio R. Barceló, who

was then president of the Liberal Party, if he knew Muñoz
Rivera.

> There was a pause in the conversation. Suddenly, I don't
> know where I got the courage, but I innocently asked
> him if he had personally known Muñoz Rivera. "Did I
> know him? Boy, perhaps better than anyone!" I asked
> him to describe how he remembered him. He lifted
> his head; he took off his thick, dark glasses; he closed
> his eyes; and he gave me an entire description of Luis
> Muñoz Rivera that was really impressive—of his face
> and body, his demeanor, how he dressed, his voice, the
> balls he had, and of his agonizingly painful, tragic, and
> premature death for the island. (73)

The second situation is a meeting between the author,
Muñoz Marín, and Lidio Cruz Monclova, a well-known historian, in which they are talking about Muñoz Rivera. Asked
a question by Muñoz Marín, the historian answers:

> LCM: Well look, Luis, I will answer you this. Muñoz
> Rivera was a headstrong, ballsy man. Certainly, when
> he finally came to an agreement about the terms of
> the pact with Sagasta and seeing that Gómez Brioso
> was reluctant to sign, he told the three Puerto Rican
> negotiators that it was essential that the three accept
> the pact. (276–277)

This language in situations of conflict or trust is not
considered appropriate in other meetings among men. In
corporations, voluntary associations (clubs, cooperatives,
etc.), boards of directors, educational institutions, groups of
professors, or professional meetings, although all may be
composed of men, the use of this language is not considered
appropriate. The members of these groups and the partici-

pants in those meetings are, for the most part, people who have a high level of schooling, possess superior linguistic abilities compared with the rest of the population, and are sufficiently able to express the same ideas in other words. They may have confrontations with, battle, and even insult each other without resorting to the language of the genitals. But these encounters are not totally exempt from such language, and the usage may arise when the group is exclusively composed of men, when the situation is loaded with tension, and the meeting is private. Those who initiate the use are in the higher levels of rank and prestige within the group.

This language of power is more common in asymmetrical relations, directed toward subordinates. It is not used in the opposite direction, from subordinate to superior, unless there is a clear intention to confront, offend, or challenge, and the use, of course, implies taking a risk. This language is also not used in the public sphere or in the media. As a rule, the language is not used in the presence of women unless extreme trust exists, the man is out of control, or the man clearly wants to offend the women.

As part of the cultural construction of male subjectivity that embodies sexuality and power in the genitals, the man pays particular attention to his penis, which is valued according to its size. From childhood, we Puerto Rican men compete on the basis of the size of our penis, and this competition continues into adulthood. The size of the penis causes great anxiety in many men, and the anxiety increases in those men who feel that theirs is small. Largeness or smallness is relative; it depends upon the man or men with which one's own is compared. Nevertheless, in the context of relativity there are some minimum requirements, and those who do not reach these minimums definitely fall into the category of men with small penises. To illustrate this point, in the homosexual environment, where large penises are highly valued, there are some well-defined standards. Penises that are less than eight inches long when erect are not considered to be large. In all cases, circumference is also considered, and a "fat" penis can compensate for its lack of length; but the ideal is to have a large and fat penis. Men who have such penises are self-satisfied, feel powerful, are inclined to boast about that fact, and, when the occasion permits, like to show off. It is a competition among men that is done intentionally, but the men are not necessarily conscious of what they are doing. For many men it is a "natural" practice, a thing men do. It is something that is expected to be done and something that has always been done. In gyms, locker rooms, and places where men appear naked, men with large penises are less inclined to cover themselves with a towel when they go to the sauna, steam room, or showers. Those with small penises generally cover themselves with a towel or underwear. It is very unusual to find a man with a small penis going around completely nude in those places. The same thing happens in public bathrooms that have many urinals lining the wall. Those who urinate standing at a distance from the urinal and seem very sure of themselves are usually men with large penises. Other men stand very close to the urinal. In some places, the following graffiti is found: *Si eres de bate corte arrímate al plato* (If you have a short bat, step closer up to the plate). Urinating at a distance from the urinal has been somewhat modified in recent years for fear of being propositioned by a homosexual. At all times, men who feel they have small penises avoid potentially embarrassing situations and having to expose them in public places. Of course, there are Puerto Rican men who have liberated themselves from this tendency, but my impression is that they make up the minority.

Urination, or *mear* (to pee) in popular language, is another component of articulation between the genitals and male power. The act is full of symbolism that transcends its physiological function. Unlike most women who sit or squat to urinate,[9] we men always have to be standing and have the penis in our hand. Urinating standing up and facing front or standing next to someone places us in a situation of power or at least of equality with regard to the other man, although men who do not feel very sure of themselves or who are afraid of being seen or of a homosexual advance distance or hide themselves from the other person or persons. García Passalacqua's (1990) narration of his encounter with former governor Muñoz Marín at the end of the fifties, when Muñoz was considered the most powerful man in Puerto Rico, is an interesting illustration of this articulation between urination and power.

> After finishing coffee and dessert and without much warning, Muñoz stood up, headed deep into the seagrape plants that were far from the table, and began to urinate. I am sure that due to a lot of scotch and wine, his new employee followed him and with great self-confidence, joined him in the process. Years later, joking while we went up the elevator in La Fortaleza to the viewpoint, he told me with a wink, "Since the time you stood beside me to pee without showing any respect, I knew that you were going to cause me problems." (106)

Clearly, the two participants in this encounter shared the same cultural code, which recognizes that the one who holds the most power is *el que más mea* (he who pisses the most). For that reason, when a Puerto Rican man humiliates, beats, or wounds an opponent, he says with much satisfaction, *Me le meé encima* (I pissed on him).

One of the dramatic events that occurred at the hearings of the notorious case of Cerro Maravilla, in which two young men who were *independentistas* were murdered by police in 1978, was the impact created on the people present by a witness who told of one of the policemen urinating on one of the cadavers after killing the young men. Undoubtedly, it was a demonstration of his power and his intent to devalue the defeated.

Puerto Rican children compete to see *quién mea más lejos* (who can pee the farthest), and the winner is the one whose stream covers the greatest distance. In a dangerous or threatening situation in which fear is felt, a person *se mea encima* (pees in his pants). Finally, in a situation in which something is easy or of little importance, *es cuestión de mear y sacudir* (it's a question of peeing and shaking). For some people the act of urinating or being urinated on is also erotic, and there was a time in which it was an act between homosexuals, although not necessarily a widespread practice. Today it still continues, if we are to believe a televised interview with a male prostitute (Esteves 1992) in which he says that it is a service requested by some clients. When the activity is not reciprocal, the one who urinates on the other is the "man," the more powerful one, the one who fits into the game of power and pleasure.

Winners and Losers

Encounters between men are based on power, competition, and possible conflict. Of course, as will be seen further on, the ability to have relationships involving camaraderie, cooperation, loyalty, and affection is not excluded; but the relationships occur within relationships of power, and it means putting those relationships before the game of power. From childhood, one learns to demand respect, to respond to aggressive situations, to defend oneself both physically and verbally, and to demonstrate invulnerability, self-sufficiency, courage, and control. We grow up in an environment that demands constant affirmation of those defining attributes of our masculinity. Masculinity is very demanding. In demonstrating masculinity, there are variations that depend on social class, religion, age group, one's physical and mental state, and reference groups, such as in the places of work, educational institutions, neighborhoods, and peer groups. Within the framework of these variations, we Puerto Rican men still share a training and a subjectivity that, although influenced by the previously mentioned differences and references, have a commonality. I agree with Rivera Medina when he says that

> the socialization and training to which the child is subjected from an early age require the suppression of any feeling that may imply weakness, frailty, fear, sensitivity, affective spontaneity; and on the contrary require learning self-destructive or high-risk answers. (1991, 18)

One of the demands of masculinity that still reigns in various sectors of Puerto Rican society and that is a basic part of the dominant ideology is that the man be the breadwinner for the family. Although there are and have been men who do not fulfill this task because of disability, incompetency, irresponsibility, or lack of skills and opportunities to have an adequate and stable income, the demand of being the breadwinner remains unaltered on an ideological plane. For example, the man is generally responsible for child support, although the current legislation maintains that both the father and mother are responsible for feeding their children,[10] and there are even women who pay child support. When the man does not comply and the woman reports him, the state penalizes him and occasionally jails him. At the present time, I have no information as to women being jailed for not paying child support. The man who is not the breadwinner, especially when he has the resources to do so, is not fully complying with one of the demands of masculinity. In this case, he is invariably branded as being irresponsible, his manliness is questioned, and he becomes *un hombre que no sirve pa ná* (a good-for-nothing man). This last statement is tempered by various situations that will be discussed below.

The existence in our society of a phenomenon that U.S. sociologists have called the "underclass" (Wilson 1990)— unemployment, underemployment, low salaries, marginalization from the working world, poverty levels, lack of necessary resources to break the circle of poverty, alcoholism and drug use among young men of productive age— prevents or at least makes it more difficult for men who belong to these sectors to comply with the demand of being a breadwinner. Sometimes their female partners do not demand that they be providers because they are aware that the men do not have the resources or because the women are the breadwinners. There are men who do not depend upon the work ethic to define their masculinity and who oppose and question masculinity. This is not to say that all men are unemployed and make no money. We should remember that some men participate in the underground economy. What is important is that a man's image, self-evaluation of his masculinity, and manifestations do not depend upon on his being a breadwinner. Nor does he lose masculinity. His masculinity remains intact when he resorts to exaggerating other male attributes, especially sexuality.

The state creates the second situation through its diverse forms of economic aid, such as food stamps, Aid to Families with Dependent Children, the Women and Infant Care program,[11] the School Meals program, and other services and subsidies that allow needy families to survive without the breadwinning father. These types of aid, which are basic for the survival of the poor population, lower the need for the man to be the main breadwinner and at the same time increase dependency on state authorities and the transfer of funds from the federal government to Puerto Rico's economy.

Third, women who become heads of household, whether it be by joining the workforce or by receiving economic aid from the state, or a combination of both, become the breadwinners for their children and, at times, for other relatives. These single mothers who are heads of household, such as those that Burgos and Colberg (1990) studied, show that women can be breadwinners. Finally, in addition to joining the workforce, women are going into fields and professions that in the past were considered to be for men and difficult for women to enter. Some less traditional women who share the economic responsibilities of the domestic group and who have been influenced by modern feminist discourses argue for more egalitarian relationships between genders. All of these situations temper the demand that the man be the breadwinner or the main breadwinner.

In a careful study of gender and class among graduate students at the Río Piedras Campus of the University of Puerto Rico, Wehbe Cabanay found that 90.5 percent of the students, both men and women, agreed with the following proposition: "The woman is the provider to the same degree as the man" (1992, 94). This finding coincides with the population's acceptance of propositions that express equality between genders. Regarding this point, Wehbe Cabanay states the following:

> The importance of the high percentage of acceptance of the propositions that express the nonacceptance of *a woman's unequal position vis-à-vis the man in the social sector composed of graduate students* can be seen in the wave effect due to the position held by the bearers of these values with respect to other social sectors (41.5% work in the economic sector or public or private education). (100–101)

At the same time that there are women breadwinners and one hears discourses on equality expressed by the graduate students that Wehbe Cabanay interviewed—discourses that are undoubtedly shared by other sectors of Puerto Rican society—the distinction between men's and women's work is still strong. Despite women's entry into jobs and professions that were male strongholds a few years ago, a high percentage of women are still in fields considered "feminine," such as teaching, nursing, and secretarial and office duties, which are low-paying occupations holding little prestige (Ostolaza Bey 1989).

Assigning men to occupations with higher prestige, decision-making power, and financial remuneration in higher numbers than women is due both to the dominance we men exercise and to the cultural or dominant ideology that states that the man should be the breadwinner, or at least the main breadwinner. This situation is accompanied by the fact that the more prestige and decision-making power in a given profession, the greater the financial remuneration. Men who are required to be the breadwinners know that they should try to obtain and keep positions that assure a higher income. Being a breadwinner gives power in the domestic sphere and prestige in the community. In addition to satisfying the needs of their families, men who earn enough to maintain lifestyles worthy of the consumer society are considered to be successful. At the same time, these men, and especially those with lower incomes, are caused great anxiety by having to be the breadwinner, and they make a great effort to try to maintain that status. On the other hand, we should be aware that prestigious and powerful jobs are limited and that most men, like women, perform routine duties. So when some feminists complain about the exclusion of women in certain jobs that "demand aggressive use of the body, physical risk, and a sense of adventure and power" (Ostolaza Bey 1989, 69), the statements seem simplistic to me because one of the hardships of masculinity is that men are assigned high-risk tasks. With the exception of the police force (which has women), whose weapons and representation of the authority of the state allow law enforcement officers to be considered an occupation of power,[12] and possibly pilots, I do not believe that the other occupations that this author mentions (firefighters, plumbers, electricians, cabinetmakers, technicians, drivers of public vehicles, mechanics) offer the "sensation of adventure and power."

Being strong, courageous, and in control of situations are other requirements of masculinity.[13] In addition to exhibiting the previous attributes, in our introductions we Puerto Rican men approach others by showing that we handle ourselves with authority and are invulnerable and respectable, which are demonstrations of the power that our masculinity bestows on us. To be accepted, which depends on the way we introduce ourselves, we have to constantly show that we possess the attributes of masculinity. That undertaking is a daily validation, and although it may be displayed in front of women, it is mainly directed toward other men—real or possible opponents in the competition to demonstrate who is more of a man. We always have to be on guard so as to not lose our masculinity or have it questioned. We must avoid being categorized as devalued, losers, or less manly; we especially do not want to be classified as a *pendejo* (jerk), *mongo* (limp), *cornudo* (horned or to be cheated on), or *maricón* (fag). Before embarking upon a discussion of these categories, I need to clarify that I am referring to encounters between men. In the spheres that are exclusively the domain of men, we men compete among ourselves to validate a constantly threatened masculinity. There is no competition between men and women in these spheres or fields of masculinity because women do not participate in them. In the framework of our subjectivity, we men do not compete with women.[14] The discussion also assumes that the encounters occur between equals, between those who hold relatively equivalent positions in terms of power, prestige, or class, or that the encounters occur in surroundings in which these differences are temporarily erased. Men who are not recognized as equals are excluded from these encounters, either because they do not possess physical or intellectual attributes, power, or economic resources to compete or because they are devalued and are therefore on the margins of masculinity.

In these encounters, in that constant competition and validation of masculinity, all Puerto Rican men who are not marginalized have to show that they are not a *mamao* (mama's boy) or a *pendejo*. This last term applies to a person "who is at the mercy of others and has lost his equality as a man" (Buitrago Ortiz 1973, 168). What Buitrago Ortiz found in Barrio Esperanza, Arecibo, in the early seventies is still a judgment shared by all Puerto Ricans. Contrary to the strong and courageous man, *el que no tiene miedo de ná* (the one who ain't afraid of nothin'), we find the type of man who is weak and afraid, the butt of jokes, not respected, called *mongo*.[15] The *mongo* does not have power and is considered disqualified to assert his positions and ideas; some men are so *mongo* that they cannot even make decisions. *Monguera* is manifested in actions that others perceive as cowardly, or in inaction. *Monguera* is also expressed in gestures, speech, the manner of walking, and body movement. The *mongo* man gives the impression that he has no control over his body or posture. He does not stand up straight. Whether he be walking, sitting, or standing, he invariably lowers his head and slumps and hunches his shoulders. He speaks slowly, as if he were searching for words, and at times he stutters. The messages he sends with his voice and body are of weakness and lethargy. The word *mongo* and its derivatives are linked with the absence of strength or power, even in the case of the *peleíta monga*, which is neither a direct confrontation nor a face-to-face fight, but resistance. Being *esmongao* is feeling worn out and weak. A *monga* is a kind of flu that weakens or incapacitates. The limp penis is *mongo*, and when an erection is lost, the man says *se me esmongó*. Finally, we should recognize that extraordinary saying of the man who articulates sexuality with power by pointing out what is physically impossible but occurs on the plane of magical realism in its Puerto Rican version: *se lo metieron mongo* (to be fucked with a limp penis). This expression means an action for which the individual was not prepared and which negatively affected him because the other person did not present himself in a threatening manner, thereby achieving his objective.

In addition to having, maintaining, and showing the attributes of masculinity, all men should be careful that their women are not unfaithful to them because that would place the men in the category of *cornudo* or *cabrón*, meaning a man who tolerates his wife's adultery. Using the phrase *pegarle cuernos* (to cheat on a person—which literally translated is "putting horns on a person") with reference to a man is a mechanism of devaluation, and in the games of power played by Puerto Rican men, accusing another man of being a *cabrón* becomes what Campbell (1966) has pointed out for the Mediterranean area as an "aggressive or secret denigration of the reputation of others" (142), which also applies to a homosexual accusation that we will discuss at length in the next chapter.

To be a man whom others respect and to be respected is another of the basic demands of our masculinity. Although respect is not exclusive to men, since women also give and demand respect, we see the demand on men with a certain particularity, because encounters between men are basically influenced by mechanisms of power; on occasion power and respect become synonymous. Our ethnology stresses the importance of respect in the enculturation of Puerto Ricans.[16] Respect is taken to mean the appropriate comportment in social encounters, in both the manner of behaving and the reaction to how others behave. As Díaz Royo points out:

> *Respeto* as a quality of comportment must be presented in face-to-face relations. It signifies proper attention to the order assumed in interpersonal relations, an acknowledgement of the other's unique soul, its individuality. (1975, 207)

Lauria (1964) offers a similar argument in his excellent analysis. Respect is a quality of the ego and is expressed in personal interactions in which each man claims his value and values the other person, and "they treat each other as if they were sacred" (56). Their value is inherent to the individual in a structured system based on inequality, but which, recognizing the existence of social and power hierarchies, affirms the dignity of each person and the necessity that this dignity be recognized by participants in social encounters. Mintz (1956) illustrates this point in his description of the relations between managers and workers in a sugarcane processing plant during the forties.

> The second *mayordomo* is unquestionably the best liked of the local managerial hierarchy. Workers say he knows how to treat them and how to show them the respect (*respeto*, not deference) they believe appropriate. Yet he himself rarely mingles with workers or tries to become their friend. (368)

A relationship of respect between men does not imply closeness or friendship, although respect is not excluded from relationships between friends and people of trust. Respect is *sui generis* and can occur in personal encounters between men who are at polar opposites of society. We inherited this relationship from agrarian society. It is a call for equal treatment by the dispossessed and subordinated vis-à-vis the powerful—a claim that asserts respect implies the reciprocal obligation of being respected. That is the reason for the emphasis on the standard of respect in the socialization of Puerto Rican children, as indicated by anthropologists who have studied agricultural communities in Puerto Rico. Díaz Royo says the following in regard to this point:

The content of the *respeto* relationship was the appropriate manner of dealing in a traditional society where powerful landlords and dispossessed *agregados* had to subsist. (1975, 209)

The importance of respect has not disappeared from Puerto Rican society. According to Fernando Picó, "In Caimito, as in other parts of Puerto Rico, children begin learning about respect very early in life" (1989, 140). A lack of respect is still considered an offense and gives rise to conflict, as illustrated by the following article from the newspaper *El Vocero*.

Convict on Probation
Kills Friend Because "He Was Not Respectful"

SAN JUAN—(By Tomás de Jesús Mangual, Staff Writer)— A well-aimed stab to the heart ended the life of Roberto Pizarro Cruz, 37, who minutes earlier had questioned the manliness of his murderer, ex-con Tomás Carrasquillo Canales, alias "Silencio."

The bloody deed occurred very early yesterday morning on 37th Street of the Parcela Falú neighborhood in Río Piedras, in the yard of the victim's home. "Silencio" and Pizarro Cruz had gone for drinks at Bar de El Cano, near the scene of the crime, and supposedly, the ex-convict did not like having Pizarro touch his backside. (De Jesús Mangual 1984, 3)

Having to comply constantly with the demands of masculinity is an arduous task, at times almost impossible. Some keep up the struggle and feel they are winners. Others retire to the fringes of masculinity and become losers. The criteria for defining a person as a winner or a loser are influenced by the social class to which a person belongs and by his reference groups. Therefore, there are variations for evaluating the relative success of each individual in being a man, and in turn, the variations are articulated with the Puerto Rican social structure.

As time goes by, after the productive and child-raising years, and with the onset of old age, the demands gradually begin decreasing. Nevertheless, the man is still expected to maintain a certain level of respect in his dealings with other men, unless mental and physical health conditions prevent him from doing so.

Competition between men is expressed by, on the one hand, proving that one has the attributes associated with masculinity and by showing that one has more attributes than one's "competitor." Contrariwise, competition also may be expressed through mechanisms of devaluation, in which one attempts to minimize the other man's masculinity and put that man in a category of "less manly," "little manly," or "not a man at all." This minimization is achieved by resorting to defamation through *chisme* (gossip) or *relajo* (joking). Taken to be the true or false information that is circulated with the intention of affecting the reputation of others, *chisme* is only associated with women in Puerto Rican society, although this is not true because *chisme* is common among men. In defamation through *chisme*, the person or persons being talked about are not present, and at times they do not find out what is being said about them. *Relajos* also refer to people who are not present, but these people are characterized as having a relationship based on family, friendship, or love with one or more of the participants in the encounter. *Careo* (confrontation) also occurs—that is, personal confrontation between the participants expressed in a complex ceremonial language that each person understands and speaks. The classic analysis of *relajos* among men is found in the work of Lauria (1964), who examined these encounters in detail as a game among men, such as jokes in which the victim of the story is directly participating in the story. The relationship of *relajo* assumes the existence of trust or a degree of intimacy between the participants. *Relajos* are not games that involve strangers; they occur in situations in which men meet during their free time, although they also occur at the workplace during breaks or when the situation allows. I have observed *relajos* in the presence of women, but women do not participate because the encounter is exclusively a masculine one. When the relationships among the participants of this game are symmetrical, anyone may begin the *relajo*. In asymmetrical relationships, the highest-ranking individual begins. Lauria makes a clear distinction between a game and a contest. In a game, the *relajo* is not taken seriously; it is just another joke. A contest, however, is a direct confrontation in which the participants become involved in a ritual of devaluation while maintaining their composure, feeling out how much each person can take without showing anger, while maintaining an air of friendliness until the confrontation ends. The encounter may turn into an aggressive confrontation or a fight, and for a fight not to occur depends upon the participants' ability to manage the ritual of degradation. In a contest, references are made to personal habits, fulfillment of obligations, political positions, and above all, sexual attributes and the use of sexuality. This type of *relajo* makes many references to the opponent's "homosexuality."[17] These encounters and the language used are influenced by class origin. In its crudest form, the encounters are displayed among men from the most subordinated sectors in class, power, and prestige structures.

Aggression, Violence, and Affectivity

Any reflection on the construction of masculinity needs to deal with aggressiveness and violence, which are terms that are generally used indiscriminately despite attempts such as Tiger's (1970) to make a differentiation. For Tiger, an anthropologist of the sociobiological tradition, aggression is defined as a process of conscious coercion against the will of an individual or group of animals or persons even when there is "no necessary element of ferocity, viciousness, or destructiveness" (201). Violence is an event that occurs within the aggressive process and is a form of participation in which one person resorts to physical force to impose his or her will over another. From Tiger's perspective, aggression, but not necessarily violence, is a part of the biological makeup of man, and aggression is loosed when men associate with each other.

> Human aggression is in part a function of the fact that hunting was vitally important to human evolution and that human aggression is typically undertaken by males in the framework of a unisexual social bond of which participants are aware and with which they are concerned. It is implied, therefore, that aggression is "instinctive" but must also occur within an explicit social context varying from culture to culture and to be learned by members of any community. (203)

The idea of biological reductionism presented by Tiger to explain male aggressiveness was widespread during the sixties, but its influence in the human sciences has decreased. The debate on whether human behavior is innate or learned is very old, and in this book it is not my intention to renew controversies that are now in the past. The biocultural dimension of human nature is the current prevailing thought. We are biological beings who at the same time are cultural; hormones, physiology, and anatomy intervene in our behaviors, but current thought is inclined to see the biological as predisposing behavior but not determinant, as Konner (1982) says in reference to the relationship between testosterone (the main male sexual hormone) and some higher levels of aggressiveness in men than in women. Along the same lines, analyzing the debate between Maccoby and Jacklin (1974) and Fausto-Sterling (1985) regarding sexual variations in the levels of aggression, Richmond-Abbot is led to the following conclusion:

> Although Maccoby and Jacklin claim that differences in aggression are found in children too young to be exposed to the socialization pressures, this claim has been disputed. Fausto-Sterling points out that in studies of children up to age 5, half the studies showed no sex-related differences, and that the observers knew the sex of the children and were looking for specific behavior. In addition, it is difficult to take into account particular cultural influences. In this culture, boys are more likely to be reinforced for aggressive behavior and thus are more likely to show it as adults. Aggression is also defined as congruent with the masculine gender role; thus males are more likely to evidence aggression rather than suppress it as females are apt to do. (1992, 53)

Without denying the biological substratum, the authors are saying that aggressiveness is considered to be associated mainly with a cultural construction. Given the fact that hunting, war, and group defense—tasks that require greater strength and involve a high risk—have traditionally been assigned to men, it is understandable that men's encultura-tion fosters the development of levels of aggression suitable for the assigned tasks. In societies that value and award winning, domination, and triumph for various activities in which competition prevails, it is not unusual for aggression to be encouraged among the members. Additionally, as Tiger says (1970), those who are motivated to meet that specific cultural demand are expected to try to act according to it.

In discussing male aggressiveness, we should avoid echo-ing extremely simplified stereotypes or descriptions of traits or behaviors of either gender. Not all men are aggressive, and not all women are passive; some women can be just as aggressive as some men, if not more. What Richmond-Abbott (1992) asserts about gender roles in the United States is applicable to modern Puerto Rican society: "Studies done to see which traits men and women actually do possess do *not* show a pattern of opposites. In reality, men and women overlap in regard to many characteristics" (6).

I feel it necessary to distinguish between aggression and violence. Taking Tiger's definition (1970) as a beginning, but excluding his biological reductionism, I take aggressiveness to be coercion, imposition, limitation, domination, or can-cellation of the other person's will. Clearly, aggressiveness must be understood in its articulation with domination and competition. Understood in this manner, aggression does not mean harm but rather control of will. Situations arise that require aggressiveness to protect or defend oneself. Aggression should also not be confused with energy. To be energetic is not the same as being aggressive, in the same way that one can be aggressive without resorting to vio-lence. Violence is an action that causes physical or emo-tional harm and is geared toward destruction or punishment, as Walter points out:

The term "violence" will be restricted to the sense of *destructive harm*. As a general term it would include not only physical assaults that damage the body, but also magic, sorcery, and the many techniques of inflicting harm by mental or emotional means. (1969, 7–8)

I am aware that differences between aggressiveness and violence can be subtle, but they do exist. Let me illustrate the difference with two everyday situations that occur in Puerto Rico.

Situation 1—Men who drive cars, especially if they are young, tend to violate traffic laws. The expected conduct on the highway is characterized by the following acts: speeding; driving under the influence of drugs or alcohol; not obeying stop signs or not paying attention to traffic lights; driving too closely behind the vehicle in front; passing in the right lane or exceedingly close to a vehicle using the technique known as the *corte de pastelillo* (zigzagging—which literally translated is a "pastry cut"); repeatedly honking the horn to make the driver in front speed up or let the car pass; driving in the emergency lane, and so on. For these and other similar reasons, drivers are cautioned to use defensive driving techniques in order to protect themselves from such aggressions, which can become violent if a crash occurs between vehicles and physical harm is done to the cars, the people, or both.

Situation 2—Two men are drinking alcohol, and one of them wants to stop drinking. The other tries to persuade him to continue and insists by resorting to phrases such as *dáte otro, acompáñame, no seas flojo* (have another, keep me company, don't be a wimp), trying to persuade him against his will. This is aggression, but for it to turn into violence, he would have to force him to drink, throw a drink in his face, or make direct references to his lack of manhood because he does not want to continue drinking.

Aggressiveness and violence in Puerto Rican society are widely documented, and a large part of this violence comes from and is encouraged by men. This fact is seen in the studies of Martínez and Silva Bonilla (1988) on sexual harassment, of Silva Bonilla (1985, 1990) on violence against women in married life, and in statistics on criminal incidence and the characteristics of the penal population. Women also resort to violence, as a recent case shows, which should not be understood as an unusual incident but rather as a frequent occurrence.

Mother Accused of Banging Baby against Crib

By Tomás de Jesús Mangual, Staff Writer, *El Vocero*

SALINAS—Sonia Vázquez Vázquez, a housewife in this town who allegedly beat her nine-month-old baby by throwing him against the crib railing to "quiet him down" when he began to cry because of colic, was accused on Monday of second degree murder and was taken to the Women's Prison of Vega Alta. Sonia, 26, showed no signs of remorse following her accusation.

The murder of the infant Gabriel Vázquez, who was not legally recognized by his father (whose whereabouts are unknown) was reported last September 8, after Sonia took him to the Health Center of this town, where she alleged that the baby was suffering from severe colic that made him cry frequently. The baby died there while being attended by doctors, and the police were notified when the doctors who saw the baby noted bruises and marks on his little body.

The case was investigated by homicide agent Héctor Dones, who, under the supervision of agent Aníbal

Soliván and District Attorney Guillermo Batlle Olivo, was able to confirm the beatings when Dr. María Conde, who performed the autopsy, determined that the infant had rib and skull fractures, and fractures on other parts of his body. Later on, agents from the Center for Criminal Investigations were able to make Sonia admit that she had beaten her newborn. (De Jesús Mangual 1992, 3, 48)

Some of men's violence is directed toward themselves or other men. In a study of violent deaths in Puerto Rico, Carnivali and Rivera found that accidents, homicides, and suicides were the main causes of death, and they calculated a rate of 59.3 deaths per 100,000 inhabitants in 1990. The authors say, "When the three different types of causes of violent deaths are taken into consideration, accidents are the leading cause. In order of importance, homicides are next and then suicides" (Carnivali and Rivera 1991, 4). Creating a profile of the characteristics of those who died from violent causes in 1987, Carnivali and Rivera discovered that most were men between the ages of 15 and 44, except for suicide cases. With respect to the suicides, they maintain that there does not appear to be "a clear and definite pattern regarding a greater incidence of suicides in specific age groups" (5). In the case of deaths by accidents, of which 56 percent were car accidents, Carnivali and Rivera state the following:

> According to 1987 data, of the three causes of violent deaths, accidents were responsible for slightly more than half (60.2 percent) of all violent deaths. A little more than three-fourths (76.6 percent) of those killed as a result of some type of accident were men, compared with 23.4 percent women. Half (50.2 percent) of

the deaths resulting from accidents occurred to people between the ages of 15 and 44. (2)

With regard to homicides:

Approximately one-fourth (25.9 percent) of all violent deaths in 1987 were homicides. The overwhelming majority (91 percent) of deaths from homicides were men. Likewise, the majority (79 percent) of homicides happened to people between the ages of 15 and 44. (3)

Suicides accounted for 14 percent of violent deaths, and as above, "Men are more prone to die from this cause of death (86 percent)" (5). According to Carnivali, death from AIDS rose 62 percent between 1988 and 1991 and is "the third leading cause of death among men." Millán Pabón's finding that "currently, 80 percent of deaths from AIDS occur in men and 20 percent in women" (1992, 18) can be added to these statistics.

The data seem to indicate that living according to the requirements of masculinity means assuming a self-destructive behavior of high risk and violence. This violence is understandable in the context of the widespread violence in Puerto Rico and an enculturation in which we men learn to be in constant competition to demonstrate that we have and maintain the attributes of masculinity. At the same time, there are few men who can show that they fulfill all the requirements demanded by the construction of gender; this "shortcoming" produces great anxiety and feelings of impotence. Men who are less able to show their control and power tend to exaggerate their masculinity. Resorting to a range of expressions of violence seems to be part of that exaggeration.

Boricuas can also show emotions, but we know very

little about our affectivity, its expressions, and its changes. To a great extent, this situation reflects the fact that the social analysis of masculinity and the discussions of masculinity carried out so far have signaled our respect, aggression, violence, and invulnerability while paying inadequate attention to other dimensions of our subjectivity. It also reflects the fact that our cultural code marks out affectivity as an emotion that should be expressed in intimate situations or situations in which there is the utmost trust. Expressing affectivity also requires that we be able to overcome the games of power implied by the masculine ideology and remove our mask of invulnerability.

4

The

Homosexual

Question

Prodigal, you have given me love
—therefore I to you give love.
O unspeakable passionate love.
—Walt Whitman

Any discussion of masculine ideology and the construction of masculinity should deal with the phenomenon of homosexuality. Historical and ethnographic evidence shows that homosexuality is a human experience that is expressed or rejected, ignored or suppressed, stamped out or encouraged, in accordance with societies' "sociosexual" assumptions.[1] Homosexuality is a sexual orientation articulated with prevailing conceptualizations of sexuality in certain societies and during specific historical periods. This means that homosexuality is not a pathological condition, an abnormality, or an aberration.[2]

I take homosexuality to be homoeroticism—erotic attraction and sexual acts between persons of the same sex.

My conceptualization of homosexuality is similar to that of other authors who have written on the subject. For Boswell, homosexuality is composed of "all sexual phenomena between persons of the same gender, whether the result of conscious preference, subliminal desire, or circumstantial exigency" (1980, 44). In his famous study on Greek homosexuality, Dover defines homosexuality as "the disposition to seek sensory pleasure through bodily contact with persons of one's own sex in preference to contact with the other sex" (1978, 1). For Ruse, homosexuals are persons who feel an erotic attraction for members of their own sex; he says that by "erotic attraction I mean (at the very minimum) fantasizing about sexual encounters; one might well feel an attraction towards someone without its being erotic" (1988, 1). I agree with Pronger (1990), who argues that we should emphasize the meanings of homosexuality, go beyond the description of behaviors, and concentrate on studying what he calls "the subjective experience." Subjective experience is taken to be the conceptualizations of our sexuality and of our sexual experiences, or the meanings that societies and individuals attribute to the domain of sexuality.[3]

Homosexuality is seen in both men and women. The female variant is called "lesbianism," while the term "homosexuality" applies specifically to erotic relations between men. In this book, I shall limit myself to discussing its male manifestation.[4]

Contrary to some people's belief that homosexuality is always a negation of masculinity, and thus relegated to the sphere of the feminine, homosexuality can be an integral part in the construction of masculinity. The statement applies both to societies that encourage the behavior and to those in which its practice is forbidden and stigmatized (among them, Puerto Rican society).

The institutionalization of berdaches, reported in 115 indigenous societies in North America at the time of their contact with European Americans, illustrates the first situation. In this case, society allows an individual biologically identified as a man to become a woman in the society and to assume the functions and symbols of the female gender without being stigmatized for doing so. This gender transformation allows berdaches to adopt women's clothing, speech, mannerisms, and occupations. They involve themselves in women's activities such as dances and even observe their rituals. Regarding berdaches, Whitehead maintains:

> Minimally, gender crossing in North America consisted of the permissibility of a person of one anatomic sex assuming part or most of the attire, occupation, and social—including marital—status of the opposite sex for an indeterminate period. The most common route to the status was to manifest, in childhood or early adolescence, behavior characteristic of the opposite sex. These manifestations were greeted by family and community with a range of responses from mild discouragement to active encouragement according to prevailing tribal sentiment, but there was seldom any question as to the meaning of certain opposite-sex-tending behaviors. (1981, 85–86)

In the case of berdaches, a male sexual relationship would be based on heterosexual patterns of gender relationships, although in some groups, it was only a partial transformation.[5]

The opposite situation—male-male sexual relationships as a part of the repertoire of expressions of sexuality and the integration of these relationships into the general process of the construction of masculinity—is illustrated in ethnographic literature by the Baruya, classical Greece of A.D. 4, and the New Guinea people known as Sambia. In all these societies, homoeroticism and sexuality in general have been widely studied.

The publication of both Dover's study (1978) on homoerotic practices as portrayed on Greek vases and Foucault's second volume of *The History of Sexuality* (1990b) generated great discussion about sexuality in the societies we have just mentioned.[6] These publications' construction of an articulation between phallocentrism, sexuality, pleasure, and power stresses the willingness of ancient Greeks to respond erotically to both sexes with no damage whatsoever to their "masculinity." The Greek citizen had several alternatives for his sexual pleasures: his wife, slaves of both sexes, strangers, and male and female prostitutes. In addition, he could become the lover of a young boy. With respect to the possibilities of sexual pleasure, Foucault says, "No sexual relation was forbidden him as a consequence of the marriage obligation he had entered into" (146). Greenberg wonders just how widespread the various sexual acts and alternatives were and argues for the possibility that eroticism was limited to certain classes.

> The extent of homosexual participation is difficult to judge. In Sparta it seems to have been universal among male citizens. In Athens, only the wealthy would have had the leisure to loiter near the gymnasia, or the wealth to purchase gifts for the adolescents they were trying to seduce. Many of the male couples depicted in Attic vase-paintings clearly belong to the urban patriciate. (Greenberg 1988, 142)

According to Foucault, eroticism is formulated around

the concept of *aphrodisia*, which he defines as "the acts, gestures, and contacts that produce a certain form of pleasure" (1990b, 40). Four aspects are especially characteristic of ancient Greek homoeroticism: (1) the celebration of beauty and the attributes of the ephebe, or young adolescent who has still not developed the physical features of an adult; (2) the idealization of the relationship between the *erastes* (adult lover) and the *eromenos* (young lover); (3) the preference for small, uncircumsized penises; and (4) the disapproval of oral sex (Griffin 1990) and penetration, which was considered an act that devalued the penetrated person. Therefore, penetration was reserved for women and inferior men (slaves and prostitutes).

In the *erastes-eromenos* relationship, we find the institutionalization and ritualization of homoerotic sexual relationships as part of the construction of masculinity in a complex articulation of pederasty, eroticism, pleasure, and power. The perfect example is the Ganymede myth.[7] The relationship was always initiated by the adult who found himself attracted to a young boy who possessed the attributes of beauty admired by the *erastes*: "broad shoulders, a deep chest, big pectoral muscles, big muscles above the hips, a slim waist, jutting buttocks and stout thighs and calves" (Dover 1978, 70). Additionally, the moral qualities of the *eromenos* were taken into consideration. The adult would begin to make advances and offer gifts; the custom was for the young boy to resist the advances and not give in too soon. When he finally agreed to begin a relationship, formalized sexual acts were begun. It was customary for the *erastes* to begin touching the young boy's chin with his left hand and his genitals with his right and then placing his penis between the boy's thighs and reaching orgasm. It was a frontal relationship; the buttocks were not touched.

The *eromenos* kept his head raised while the *erastes* buried his against the boy's chest. The young boy was expected to be tolerant of his lover's sexual advances and to satisfy his desires without showing pleasure or excitation. According to Keuls (1985), emotional bonds did develop in these relationships. Ideally, the adult became a kind of mentor to the young boy with respect to this aspect of the relationships. Greenberg has the following to say:

> The older partner in a pederastic relationship strove to win the admiration and love of the younger through exemplary conduct, while the younger sought to emulate the older. Sex thus served to prepare young men for adulthood. In Sparta this pedagogic function was heavily militarized, while in Athens it involved preparation for the more varied life of an Athenian adult. (1988, 148)

The participants would belong to the same social class, and as time passed, the *eromenos* would become an *erastes*. There is always a lingering question whether ideal sexuality, as it appeared on vases and in books, corresponded to everyday practice.[8]

In the New Guinea society known as Sambia (Herdt 1981), children between the ages of seven and ten are separated from their mothers, and the world of women in general, and are subjected to elaborate rituals of initiation into manhood that last approximately seven years. Originally, the Sambians had been a warrior society, but they had been pacified by Australians during the colonial administration. In spite of the forced pacification, the idea of masculinity continues to be associated with warrior attributes. Men were expected be strong, courageous, and reliable in fulfilling their tasks. The distinguishing feature of masculinity is strength, but a man is not born with strength; he must acquire it through the initiation rituals. With respect to the meaning of strength, Herdt says the following:

> A man is the sum of his forceful vitality or strength (*jerungdu*) and masculine behaviors. Strength is a product of heritage and semen and successive initiations, so it is synonymous with masculinity itself. And from strength comes manhood. Manhood can be observed: in one's proud bearing, fighting prowess, abilities to trap game and, from sheer muscle, to clear wild tracts of rain forest. A manly man knows how to perform painful rituals on himself and how to handle his wife and estate. (1981, 203)

The initiate acquires strength from other men by swallowing semen in an initiation process of ritualized homoeroticism that makes him a man. The process of going from boy to man consists of seven stages. In the first stage, the boy (7–10 years old) is separated from his mother and is taken to live in the men's house, where he is forced to practice oral sex as the receptor of another young boy's semen. The boy who is orally penetrating the initiate and providing semen is another youngster, who is in the final stages of the initiation process. In the second stage (ages 10–13), the initiates continue ingesting semen and living in the collectivity of the men's house, and in the third stage they become penetrators and providers of semen to new initiates. In the fourth and fifth stages (16–17+), some of the initiation rituals, among them marriage, are public and are celebrated in the villages. Secretly, married men instruct new husbands in sexual practices with women. At the beginning of the marriage and until the wives have had their first menstruation, recently married men continue acting as penetrators in oral relations with both their wives and the initiates who live in the men's house. Beginning coitus with their wives signals the start of the sixth stage (20–30), in which the men acquire the status of adults, and their homoerotic practices end. The adult Sambian becomes what is known in other societies as a completely heterosexual man. As among the Baruya, a man who penetrates a woman vaginally cannot put his penis in a young initiate's mouth because it will contaminate the youth.[9]

Sinners, Criminals, the "Sick"

The trial of the famous writer Oscar Wilde in England in 1895, in which Wilde was found guilty of sodomy and sentenced to prison,[10] is considered a watershed in criminalizing the practice of homoeroticism in the British Empire and nations under imperial influence (Greenberg 1988; Hyde 1970; Ruse 1988). Unlike other European nations and several Latin American societies that—inspired by French law and the adoption of the Napoleonic Code—decriminalized homosexuality in the nineteenth century, the English retained homosexuality as a criminal offense until 1967. With the passing of the Sexual Offences Act that year, private homosexual acts between consenting adults became legal in England and Wales, although the legislation did not apply to Scotland and Northern Ireland (Hyde 1970, 268–269).

The criminalization of sexual acts between men in Western societies was one of many events associated with the transition toward modernity and with the abandonment of medieval European mentalities, practices, and laws. During the period of European feudalism, the conceptualizations of sexuality in general, and homoeroticism in particular, that informed Christian morals and the positions taken by the church were the result of a long process begun when the primitive Christian church took a disliking to the sexual expressions of Greco-Roman eroticism and declared sexual intercourse acceptable only for purposes of procreation (Greenberg 1988, 228). The church became antagonistic toward homoeroticism, which gradually became defined as sodomy, an act *contra natura*, and sinful.[11] About this change, Greenberg says the following:

> By the year 1300, Europe had become distinctly less hospitable to those who engaged in homosexual acts than it had been two hundred years earlier. Philosophy, theology, and literature of the late Middle Ages display a dread of homosexuality; canon law was antagonistic, and secular law highly repressive. (279)

By the eighteenth century, the prohibition of sodomy in medieval society had changed to the condemnation of perversion and criminalization of homoeroticism through a process that Foucault (1990a) calls an "incorporation of perversions." As a result, "peripheral sexualities" are persecuted, namely, those that deviate from heterosexual norms and are found at the margins of society. For Foucault:

> This new persecution of the peripheral sexualities entailed an *incorporation of perversions* and a new *specification of individuals.* As defined by the ancient civil or canonical codes, sodomy was a category of forbidden acts; their perpetrator was nothing more than the juridical subject of them. The nineteenth-century homosexual became a personage, a past, a case history, and a childhood, in addition to being a type of life, a life form, and a morphology, with an indiscreet anatomy and possibly a mysterious physiology. (42–43)

The criminalization of homosexuality—whereby male-male sexual intercourse is considered an illegal act and subject to legal prosecution—that began with the development of modern state societies remains unaltered in several states in the United States and in Puerto Rico. The debate about the legality or illegality of such acts and the reluctance in the United States to decriminalize homosexual intercourse intensified in 1986, when the United States Supreme Court refused to overturn a Georgia state law making sodomy a crime. The law prohibits male-male anal intercourse, even if done between adults of their own free will, and in total privacy (Ruse 1988, 236). In addition, that other societies have decriminalized homosexuality does not necessarily mean that it is accepted or tolerated. Homophobia, persecution, stigmatization, and devaluation of homosexuals continue in most modern societies. Homosexuality is stigmatized when it is rejected, condemned, or devaluated, and also when it is designated as a dishonorable sexuality or as a disgrace to both those who practice it and the people who are close to homosexuals. Stigmatization of homosexuality is consistent with a dominant sexual ideology, which favors heterosexuality and condemns deviant sexual expressions. Therefore, these expressions become what Foucault calls "peripheral sexualities." They are considered peripheral because they are found on the fringes of society, in that marginality to which societies relegate all those types of expressions, acts, and ideas that enjoy neither the majority's approval nor the institutional endorsement of church and state.

Another effect of the modern age in the conceptualization of homosexuality was made through (1) homosexuality's medicalization and (2) the dichotomization of male sexuality into the components of heterosexuality versus homosexuality. As was mentioned in the part of book that discusses the construction of masculinity, these categories did not exist, and do not now exist, in societies in which eroticism between men forms a part of the expressions of sexuality. Conceiving homoerotic orientation as a sickness did not signify a liberating approach in the general climate of homosexual oppression. The excellent analyses of this process by both Greenberg (1988) and Ruse (1988) show that the actual effect of this conception was the transfer of a power that in earlier ages was held by ecclesiastical and civil authorities to the medical profession, which then was allowed to evaluate and make decisions about homosexuals. Sinners, criminals, or "sick": What difference does it make?[12] I refer to the fact that living with a sexual orientation that is devalued, condemned, and stigmatized, irrespective of the categories used to conceptualize it, has disastrous consequences for the individual. Being looked upon as a sinner, a criminal, or a person who is mentally ill means dealing with rejection, ridicule, a sense of guilt, contempt, and even physical violence on a daily basis, as we shall see in a few pages when we look at the expressions of homosexuality in Puerto Rico and its articulation with the construction of masculinity. All of these issues have great implications for self-esteem, acceptance of one's own sexuality, male-female relationships, and, finally, how a person situates himself/herself in social and sexual encounters with persons of the same or opposite sex.

One issue in the medicalization of homosexuality is the argument that homosexuality has a genetic basis, and thus that its expression is regulated by biological mechanisms. The explanation of homosexuality as an innate condition dates from the ancient Greeks: it was argued for during the Middle Ages and has acquired great significance in modern times (Greenberg 1988, 404).[13] This debate has not been resolved, and to date there is no definitive or unquestionable evidence or proof that homosexuality—taken to be a sexual preference for persons of one's own sex, and characteristic of a minority of men—is an innate condition. Studies aimed at proving the biological basis of sexual orientation, among them LeVay's (1991), which was published in the prestigious magazine *Science*, have not been able to show that there are fundamental biological differences between homosexuals and heterosexuals.

LeVay is a neuroscientist who studied a region of the brain known as the anterior hypothalamus, which, according to other research, is involved in regulating typically masculine or heterosexual sexual behavior in primates. He cites other researchers who have found that in the hypothalamus of men and women "of unknown sexual orientation" (1035) there are two groups of neurons, INAH 2 and INAH 3, that are significantly larger in men than women. The main objective of LeVay's research was to test his hypothesis that variations in the size of one or both groups of neurons is associated with sexual orientation. With respect to this point, LeVay says the following:

> Specifically, I hypothesized that INAH 2 or INAH 3 is large in individuals sexually oriented toward women (heterosexual men and homosexual women) and small in individuals sexually oriented toward men (heterosexual women and homosexual men). Because tissue from homosexual women could not be obtained, however, only that part of the hypothesis relating to sexual orientation in men could be tested. (1035)

LeVay analyzed brain tissue obtained in the autopsies of 41 individuals who died in hospitals in New York and

California. Nineteen men were identified as homosexuals who died of complications related to the AIDS virus. There were 16 heterosexual men, of whom 6 also died from AIDS-related complications, and 6 heterosexual women. Measuring the volume of the four cell groups found in that region of the brain, LeVay found that the neurons identified as INAH 3 were larger in the heterosexual men than in the women and the homosexual men. Although he found that there was a difference in the size of those cells, he was very cautious in his interpretation of the results, and he concludes by saying that

> the results do not allow one to decide if the size of INAH 3 in an individual is the cause or consequence of that individual's sexual orientation, or if the size of the INAH and sexual orientation covary under the influence of some third, unidentified variable. (1036)

Another current debate among the scholars of human sexuality is the controversy between the "essentialists" and "social constructionists" with respect to the nature of sexual orientation, and the positions that the two groups take when addressing the categories of "heterosexual," "homosexual," and "bisexual." Essentialists "treat sexuality as a biological force and consider sexual identities to be cognitive realizations of genuine, underlying differences" (Epstein 1992, 241). They also accept the legitimacy of the categories named above and apply them in their studies, because they feel that a person's sexual orientation is the manifestation of objective and inherent differences, which are also independent of culture. The basic premises of "essentialists" are summarized by Boswell:

> Humans are differentiated at an individual level in terms of erotic attraction, so that some are more

attracted sexually to their own gender, some to the opposite gender, and some to both, in all cultures. (1992, 137)

We constructionists, however, maintain that there are no such inherent differences. In our view, sexual orientation is expressed in the context of a person's social construction, and the significances of sexuality are articulated with culture and history. For us, the categories of "heterosexual," "homosexual," or "bisexual" are arbitrary; they are labels that acknowledge neither the complexity of the development of sexual identity nor variations in the expressions of human sexuality.

El Ambiente, or the World of Homosexuality in Puerto Rico

Homosexuality in Puerto Rico is seen variously as a sinful act, a crime, a sickness, or a sexual orientation, depending upon the ideological stance that the individual, social group, or institution assumes in dealing with homosexuality. We have no information that allows us to arrive at definite conclusions about the levels of tolerance or intolerance toward homosexuality,[14] although the prevailing social climate tends toward stigmatization and current law penalizes male-male sexual intercourse.[15]

Despite its repudiation, rejection, and condemnation, homoeroticism is one expression of Puerto Ricans' sexuality. Sexual encounters between men are part of daily life as it is articulated with pleasure, adventure, fear, denials, momentary remorse, and power. The recognition of the existence of homosexuality is illustrated in the binary opposition of the "real man" and "non-man" categories, a basic part of the Puerto Rican's socialization in the parameters of masculinity, and part, too, of the constant show of masculinity in every aspect in our daily life. In contrast to the real man, the macho—what every man should be—there is what a man should not be, the non-man or *maricón* (fairy). The *maricón* is the total negation of masculinity, an individual who is devalued and despised, and calling a man *maricón* is the worst insult that could ever be given him.[16] The word is so offensive that when one homosexual wants to humiliate another, he calls him *maricón*. If the intention is to strengthen the insult further, he will call him *maricona* or *mariquita* to remove the most minimal vestige of masculinity that he may have and place him in the sphere of the feminine. The most dejected, devalued, and despised of Puerto Rican men, about whom it is said that *no vale ná* (ain't worth nothin'), consider themselves superior to a *maricón*. The worst misfortune for a man is that a son should *salirle pato* (turn out to be a fairy). A *mariconería* is a devalued act or object that merits ridicule. Men's small purses are called *mariconeras*. Continuing in this manner, a complex articulation—which is a significant component of the dominant ideology in Puerto Rico—with masculinity, courage, and power is constructed in opposition to nonmasculinity, devaluation, and powerlessness. This ideology permeates male-female and same-sex relationships and is manifested daily, however contradictory it may seem, even in *el ambiente* (world of homosexuality) in Puerto Rico.

El ambiente is as heterogeneous, diverse, and complex as the world of heterosexuality, from which *el ambiente* is not completely segregated. The two worlds cross each other constantly in family relations, workplaces, schools and other institutions, malls, hangouts, squares, streets, and neighborhoods. Very few people in Puerto Rico live in a completely homosexual world. Homosexual exclusivity is found in centers for recreation and fraternization, such as certain bars, discos, guest houses, and some beaches. There are also urban areas that are specifically designated as meeting spots, to which men go at certain times with the sole purpose of making contacts to have sex. There are also other places that are known as "mixed," such as bars, pool halls, and gyms in which the clientele is mostly men. At these places, contacts are made for sex, while each person maintains his heterosexual mask. As will be discussed later in further detail, some men involved in these encounters do not consider themselves homosexuals. In some towns in Puerto Rico where there are no gay bars, contacts are made in these latter types of places. Generally speaking, any space in which men congregate is a possible meeting center, which does not imply that all Puerto Rican men are willing to participate in homosexual relations.

The differentiation and complexity of *el ambiente* stem from the fact that *el ambiente* reflects all the mind-sets that exist in modern Puerto Rico. In *el ambiente*, we find the same political ideologies and partisan positions as in the rest of society. There are also atheists, agnostics, and every sort of religious belief from conservative Catholicism to spiritualism and santería, with the exception of priests and nuns who take a vow of chastity and members of fundamentalist Protestant sects, for whom homosexuality is a sin and the work of the devil.[17] *El ambiente* reproduces class differences and class ideology. Racism exists, although its participants display the same phenotypical variations as the rest of the population. There are people of all ages, with the exception of prepubescent boys and old men who have lost interest in sex. We find both the consumer ideology and the cult of youth and physical beauty that pervade the rest of society.

Three factors make up the specificity of *el ambiente*: (1) the sexual preference of its participants is mostly oriented toward persons of the same sex; (2) the high valuation of large penises, to the point that this value surpasses any other criteria of desirable physical attributes; (3) a cult of masculinity that reproduces the dominant masculine ideology in a contradictory manner.

El ambiente's own internal differentiation—the differentiation that is specific to itself and comes before the distinctions among human beings that Puerto Rican society has established (color, class, gender, power, etc.)—is articulated with forms that one takes on in order to reproduce the masculine ideology in *el ambiente*. I call it a contradictory reproduction because *el ambiente* accepts, praises, and transforms those attributes and symbols of masculinity constructed around power that were discussed in the previous chapter. The same power that devalues and looks down on women and homosexuals is eroticized in male-male sexual intercourse and becomes the base on which homoeroticism is constructed.[18] The discourses of homosexuality in Puerto Rico celebrate the materialization of power in the genitals, a man's physical strength and courage, his eroticism, and other attributes that glorify the masculine figure. Around these discourses, categories are constructed to fit the diversity of orientations, fantasies, and sexual preferences in *el ambiente*; likewise, a general category is created for those who do not participate in *el ambiente*. The categories are the following:

Straight:[19] "Straight" people are heterosexuals who neither know about *el ambiente* nor take any part in it; they live their lives at a complete distance from the homosexual world.

Entendido: This category designates heterosexuals who

know about *el ambiente*, spend time socially with homosexual individuals or groups, and are not homophobes. Their level of participation in *el ambiente* varies from having some knowledge about it to having a complete understanding of its diversity and complexity, in addition to being more involved in activities of homosexual groups. The *entendido* may have occasional sex with men but does not consider himself to be a homosexual, and others do not label him as one either. Some *entendidos* do not have homoerotic relations.

Ponca: A *ponca* is someone who acts heterosexual, but the people in *el ambiente* do not acknowledge his claim of masculinity. He is suspected of having or of having had sexual intercourse with other men in which he is or was orally or anally penetrated; thus, he is disqualified as a man because in Puerto Rico a penetrated man loses his masculinity. The way he carries his body, his manner of walking, the tone of his voice, his look, and his attitudes toward homosexuals send messages that are not received as masculine. The *ponca* does not inspire confidence because he is considered a homophobe and in his eagerness to pass as a man may be capable of "outing" others. Unlike the *loca del closet* (closet queen), about whom no doubt exists with respect to his homosexuality, even though he may not be involved in *el ambiente* or have homoerotic relations, no proof is needed of a *ponca*'s homosexuality; suspicion is enough.[20]

Bugarrón: The *bugarrón* is a man who considers himself to be heterosexual, a claim that is not questioned even if he is involved in *ambiente* activities and has sex with men whose masculinity he does not recognize and whom he calls *loca* (gay), *mujer* (woman), *mami* (momma), or *mamita* (little momma). In his physical appearance, voice, dress, and gestures, the *bugarrón* incorporates and exaggerates all of the distinguishing characteristics of the Puerto Rican male. During sex, he is always the penetrator, both oral and anal. His usage of sexuality is highly ritualized to conserve his manhood and avoid being questioned about it. Any exchange or violation of rituals by the sex partner is punishable, and the *bugarrón* has no qualms about resorting to physical aggression to defend his male image. The ritualization of the *bugarrón*'s sexuality, in addition to his always being the penetrator, is expressed in the following acts: he may not kiss the other person or allow the other person to kiss him on the mouth or face; he does not allow his face or buttocks to be touched; only the front part of the body between his neck and thighs may be touched; some *bugarrones* allow only the penis and testicles to be touched; and he will never touch the other person's genitals. Although the *bugarrón* may allow himself to touch his partner's buttocks, not all do. The strict observance of these rules of the games is essential to be able to have sex with a *bugarrón*. His sex partners have to assume an attitude that appears subordinate and feminine in gestures, speech, and in any social and sexual interactions. Some *bugarrones* who have relationships of relative stability with a *loca*, after developing much trust, will allow some of the rules to be violated, as long as the violation is always kept in total secrecy. Sex with *bugarrones* requires payment, whether it be in money, favors, alcohol, food, drugs, gifts, or a combination of these. If they regularly visit or live with a *loca*, some *bugarrones* are completely supported. Some have more or less stable jobs, and others work sporadically or live totally off their bodies. *Bugarrones* belong to a well-defined class sector; they come from the working class or the underclass. They have little schooling and limited skills in the working world. As many of them say, they are street-smart. Many are alcoholics or drug addicts. They live their lives on the borders between legality and illegality. Invariably, *bugarrones* are young and have some physical appeal that is valued in *el ambiente*, such as large penises and a manly bearing; they know how to use their sexuality to their advantage. After reaching a certain age, when they begin to lose their looks, if they are not dead or in jail, they retire to live with women or integrate into *el ambiente* as homosexuals; some devote their lives to fundamentalist religions, feeling remorse for the lives they led.

Loca: Any man who is known to be a homosexual by the people of *el ambiente* is called a *loca*; he himself considers himself as homosexual, and during sex he takes the position of the penetrated, whether it be anally, orally, or both ways. His sexual preference may be to act as the penetrator, but he lets himself be penetrated by others. Others enjoy both positions equally. There are also *locas* who limit their sexual repertoire to being the penetrated, and they are known as *locas* who are *bien pasivas* (very passive). This category is the most complex and most diverse. It is made up of a very heterogeneous population that differs in at least six main characteristics: (1) the degree of acceptance of his own sexuality; (2) the level of participation in *el ambiente*; (3) sexual preferences; (4) gestures, bearing, dress, in addition to position and presentation in the continuum associated with the masculine-effeminate feminine; (5) color, class, education, and occupation; and (6) place of residence.

The degree of recognition of one's own homosexuality ranges from complete acceptance—and the resulting adoption of a lifestyle consistent with the conceptualization of the individual and his reference groups with respect to what it is that makes one homosexual—to denial. The conflictive and contradictory process of acceptance-denial, which every individual with homoerotic inclinations goes through, begins to crystallize after "coming out of the closet." This is a kind of debut that is not necessarily related to a man's first homoerotic sexual experiences. Coming out is the start of the acquisition of understanding of *el ambiente*—its rules, games, symbols, values, and language. Involvement in *el ambiente* includes both social activities and sexual experimentation and having amorous flings or relatively permanent relationships. The stage when one comes out of the closet also varies. Some men come out when they are teenagers, while others need more time; there are men who come out when they are mature adults bordering on old age. Some come out without having had sexual experiences with persons of the opposite sex, while others do so after being married, having children, and fulfilling the demands of heterosexuality that society imposes. Some never come out, but by exhibiting attributes associated with homosexuals, they become classified as such and are called *locas del closet*.[21] Others go in and come out of the closet at different stages during their lives. Although coming out is associated to a large degree with the recognition of one's own homoerotic inclination, it does not mean that the conflict between acceptance and denial has been completely resolved. Likewise, a man can have sexual intercourse with men and enjoy being penetrated without accepting that he is homosexual. Denial of homoerotic sexual orientation and the feeling of guilt and shame that is felt have to be understood in the context of a society that favors heterosexuality and consequently penalizes, devalues, and ridicules other sexualities.

The level of participation in *el ambiente* and in social and sexual encounters or their combination is not uniform; it may change throughout a person's life. While some men live in an almost exclusively homosexual world, others maintain more of a distance. Living completely in *el ambiente* means having limited voluntary contact with heterosexuals, for example, when it is impossible not to meet one's minimal responsibilities to the family or the working world. It also means having a social life in which one's interaction is mostly with other homosexuals, in which one goes frequently to bars, beaches, discos, and meeting spots. Other men limit their social encounters or are not involved in them but have an active sex life. We likewise find individuals who are very removed from *el ambiente*, although they consider themselves to be a part of it.

Sexual preferences within the same sex cover a wide range of practices that are articulated with the eroticization and the reproduction of masculinity and with how each person sees himself in that complex continuum that ranges from the most "real man" to the least "real man." Therefore, we find persons who limit their preferences to specific acts with others who have certain attributes that they consider to be erotic. This is the case, for example, of those who only allow themselves to be penetrated by *bugarrones* or by homosexuals who act very manly and pass for heterosexuals. In turn, there are those who look for effeminate individuals in order to penetrate them. Between these two extremes can be found an ever changing repertoire of sexual acts with various types of people. Some look for men with mannerisms tending toward the feminine; others prefer men with a more manly bearing, or as they say in *el ambiente*, *que no tengan plumas* (they don't have feathers). Some men prefer young men under the age of twenty. Others are attracted to mature men over forty. Some like black men, while others like white men.[22] There are those who look for men with little or no body hair, and others who are crazy about men with a lot of body hair. Those who are not very discriminating about physical characteristics or specific sexual acts may have a wide repertoire of partners and experiences. In short, erotism in *el ambiente* is varied and complex.

The contrast between the man and non-man is manifested on a continuum of expressions and representations that range from very masculine, through the effeminate, to the feminine. Every person, measured by his gestures, bearing, dress, tone and modulation of voice, can be located somewhere along this continuum. At one extreme is the *bugarrón* with his exaggeration and vulgarization of masculinity, and at the other are those men who dress like women and act as if they were women. Between these two extremes we find great diversity in how each person acts and expects to be acknowledged, which is very closely tied to his social standing and background. The higher in the ranks of class, color, power, and occupation, the more we find a tendency to present a manly bearing, at least in public. In those circles, *locas vestidas* (drag queens), who are men who dress like women, or *locas partidas*, who are men who look too effeminate, are not accepted. *Locas partidas* are seen more frequently in the lower strata of the social classes.

In addition, *el ambiente* is not homogeneous with respect to color and class. In it are found people who represent the entire spectrum of phenotypes and social classes of the Puerto Rican population, from those who live on the margins of society in public housing and shantytowns to those in high society. This does not mean that in *el ambiente* class differences, color, and prestige disappear or are erased. On the contrary, racism and classism do exist and are constantly manifested. Public places such as bars, discos, and clubs are subtly segregated by generation and by distinctions in the continuum of class and color. Segregation is more visible in places of social and sexual encounters that are private or by invitation only, such as homes, beach houses, boats, and country houses. It is true that sexual encounters occur between people from different social and color ranks, but that does not mean that these are relationships of relative equality. Such encounters are nuanced by subtle differences and are played out in complicated games of power and pleasure. Social and color differences are eroticized to the point that there are *locas* in the bourgeoisie with pretensions to aristocracy who sexually prefer those who are marginalized. Others sarcastically sing the following refrain to the *locas de la burguesía*: *Dama, dama. De alta cuna y de baja cama* (Lady, lady, from a high crib to a low bed).[23] The same diversity is found in the levels of education, occupation, and places of residence. Although there are occupations stigmatized as being for homosexuals, such as florists, makeup artists, nurses, ballet dancers, and interior decorators, there are men in these professions who are not homosexuals. In turn, we find homosexuals in professions that have traditionally been heterosexual strongholds, such as medicine, engineering, and law. In Puerto Rico there are no communities or neighborhoods that are characterized as having a high percentage of people from *el ambiente*, as is the case of the Village in New York, Newtown in Chicago, and the Castro District in San Francisco. Puerto Rico's homosexuals are all over the island and are found in public housing developments, shantytowns, *parcelas* (government-distributed plots of land), subdivisions, and condominiums. Only an empirical study of living patterns can answer how they are distributed in different neighborhoods.

Gay

In the late sixties and early seventies, the category of "gay" began to be incorporated into *el ambiente* of Puerto Rico. This term came from the United States, where its use dates from the fifties.[24] In the seventies, the popularity of this category in the United States was articulated with the development of social movements that rebelled against the prevailing social order. Many of the movements took a position that broke with the dominant ideologies; they began to propose changes in social structures and the prevailing mind-sets, while they simultaneously developed modes of coexistence and a daily life that articulated ideas with practice. Hippies, communes, sexual liberators, the civil rights movement, the antiwar movement, urban riots, ecological groups, Woodstock, and especially Stonewall were influential in and contributed to creating a new movement committed to working for gay rights in the late sixties known generically as "Gay Liberation."[25] A communitarian and political militancy began that used the category of gay as the symbol of a new consciousness. Proud, assertive stances were taken in support of homoeroticism as a legitimate sexual orientation, and the principles of the new gay culture were established.[26] "The love that dare not speak its name" took to the street; "homosexual (the private and secret) changes to gay (the public and open)" (Herdt 1992, 11). Being gay is seen as a new orientation that goes beyond sexual acts. It is a conscious decision, a set of beliefs, symbols, experiences, and a mind-set that celebrates and supports eroticism with the same sex. According to Herdt, "It means repudiation and symbolic transformation of the stigmata of homosexuality—in the psyche and in the world" (59).

Whether by mimicry or awareness, the new category

was popularized in *el ambiente* in Puerto Rico during the seventies. On August 5, 1974, in San Juan, a group of gay men and lesbians founded the Comunidad de Orgullo Gay (the Gay Pride Community, or COG, as it is known in Spanish), which helped to implement the use of the category.[27] Today, the category of "gay" is very widespread in *el ambiente* and is taking the place of the *loca*, although it has not completed replaced it. Generally, the term tends to be used by homosexuals from the upper and middle classes who came out when the term began to be used in Puerto Rico or after its use became widespread. The term "gay" lacks the pejorative and humiliating connotations that are associated with *maricón*, *pato*, and *loca*. It also does not have the technical and clinical meaning of "homosexual." It is easier to be accepted as a gay person. People who call themselves "gay" are not necessarily saying that they have developed a new awareness and a rebellious stance against the dominant masculine ideology.

The absence of open and aggressive discrimination and repression against gay people on the part of the state and civil society may give some readers the impression that Puerto Ricans live in a society that accepts or tolerates homoeroticism. Contrary to this position, I maintain that sexism and homophobia are manifested daily in Puerto Rican society and that collectively, homosexuality is not accepted as a legitimate sexual orientation or preference. In the public sphere, society tries to hide or conceal homophobia, as it does with racism. In private situations, among people of trust, it is another story. Homophobia has traditionally been explained as an irrational fear of homosexuality. This explanation is limited because it does not consider homophobia to be one of the components in exercising power. In line with Pronger (1990), I also maintain that homophobia in men is due to their fear of being penetrated and having their frailty, which the heterosexual mask hides, uncovered.[28] In Puerto Rican society, penetration and frailty are associated with a lack of power. In this context, the exclusion of openly gay men from positions of power, whether elected or appointed positions, can be understood. Accepting someone who is gay, a penetrated person, a *maricón* (call him what you will), into a position of power means weakening the bases of the power of masculinity and the privileges of heterosexuality. In Puerto Rico, the relative tolerance of homosexuality ends when an openly gay person aspires to or obtains a position of power. At that moment, homophobia is violently unleashed.

In conclusion, *el ambiente* has not gone beyond the masculine ideology's games and forces of power. Although at an individual level we find persons who are relatively liberated from that ideology, these same people also daily confront the reproduction of that ideology in discourses of power, pleasure, and pain: the power of conquering or being conquered; the power of manipulating another person, which is seen in sex games to find out who has control; the pleasure of erotic encounters and of discovering a partner's sexuality; the pleasure of penetrating or being penetrated. There is the enjoyment of male bodies in a sexuality that, being stigmatized by society, is expressed in a climate of secrecy and clandestineness in which the prohibition exacerbates the pleasure. In addition, there is the pain that is caused by feeling less manly, the constant threat of devaluation, and the absence or loss of the physical attributes that are valued in *el ambiente*; the pain of rejections, which leads to passing flings and the constant search for pleasure. There is the pain of those men who do not find their prince charming. And finally, there exists the very specific pain that is felt by those who have never been loved by another man.

5

Toward

a New

Masculinity

Traveler, there is no path.
You make it as you go forward.
—Antonio Machado

The central topics of this book are, first, power and its articulation with sexuality, and second, privileges and demands of masculinity. Power has traditionally been taken to mean the ability to dominate, censure, suppress, exercise control over, or subordinate the acts and wishes of others who do not have power. From this viewpoint, power demands obedience and assumes the ability to punish those who resist power or do not act in accordance with the wishes and mandates of those who have power and exercise it. Some people's powers lie in others' lack of power. Power is either had or not had, is taken or not, is conserved or is lost, is exercised or not—but is never shared. Many of these conceptualizations about power have been formulated in the context of the state—its institutions and mechanisms—on the basis of Weber's classic definition, "We understand by power the chance of a man or of a number of men to realize their own will in a communal action or even against the resistance of others who are participating in the action" (1958, 180).

The concept of power that I use in this book is based on Foucault's definition (1990a) more than Weber's. Foucault maintains that power is not a privilege of a dominant group that is exerted over the dominated. For Foucault, power is neither unitary nor exclusive to an individual or group. On the contrary, Foucault says that power is "immanent," by which he means to say that it arises from human relations structured on the basis of principles of inequality. For him, relations of power are a product of the "divisions, inequalities, and disequilibriums" in social relations. Foucault also tells us that power is omnipresent, that it is exercised "in every relation from one point to another" (93). This means that "power is everywhere" (93) and is manifested daily in all our relations. According to Moore, this argument "is, I think, a familiar one in anthropology, because anthropologists are acquainted with the diffuse and immanent nature of power relations in small-scale societies which lack formalised offices, stations, and bureaucracies" (1986, 194). For Foucault, the dominated are also active beings in the production and reproduction of power relations; thus, he says that "power comes from below." Finally, Foucault states that "where there is power, there is resistance," an opposition that arises from those same relations and that may be expressed in many ways. In short, Foucault believes that power is composed of four principal elements: (1) the multiplicity of force; (2) the process that transforms, strengthens, or reverses these force relations; (3) the support that these force relations find in one another; (4) the strategies in which they take effect (92–93).

Based on Foucault's postulate that where there is power there is resistance, we can state that in any society in which the masculine ideology is dominant, we will find many types of resistance toward that ideology, irrespective of their effectiveness or lack thereof in transforming the power relations created by gender divisions. Currently, in addition to the traditional kinds of resistance, a feminist discourse has been articulated that in its heterogeneity shares the questioning and open confrontation of the powers and privileges of masculinity. In this rebellious discourse, new ways of constructing male-female relationships are outlined. The challenge to the power of masculinity presented both by feminist movements and by gay culture have led some men to reflect upon and question the parameters of masculinity. Additionally, some men have become aware that the masculine ideology also oppresses them and that by reproducing this ideology on a daily basis, we men become our own oppressors. As a result of these processes, men's movements are beginning to be organized in order to reflect on their masculinities and question the possibility of constructing a new masculinity that is not based on power, competition, and domination.

In the United States, Bly (1990) and Keen (1992) have written popular books that are oriented toward examining the modern concept of masculinity and that offer alternatives for its transformation. Both have had certain repercussions in Puerto Rico.

Bly's book revolves around two main topics. The first of these is the absent father and the need that we men have to be reunited with the paternal figure. The second topic is the exploration of the positive aspects of masculinity—its

creative and sustaining masculinity. Bly develops these topics with the narration of one of the Grimm Brothers' fairy
tales based on a character named Iron John.

The story begins with the strange events that happen in
an area of the forest near a king's castle. Hunters who went
into the forest would never came out again. For many years,
no one would dare enter the forest, until one day a hunter
arrived and offered to go in. He went in with his dog. As
soon as the dog began pursuing game, it became stuck be-
side a deep pool. A hand came out of the pool, grabbed the
dog, and pulled it into the depths of the water. The hunter
returned to the castle and rounded up several men who
helped him empty the pool. When they reached the bot-
tom, they found a Wild Man whose body was the color of
rusted iron and who had hair that reached down to his knees.
The hunter and his group tied this man up and took him to
the castle. The king locked him in a cage in the courtyard
of the castle, forbade anyone from opening the cage, and
gave the key to the queen. A few years later, the king's son
was playing with a golden ball that rolled into the Wild Man's
cage. The Wild Man refused to return the boy's ball. He told
the boy that he would return it if he opened the cage with the
key that the queen kept under her pillow. The boy stole
the key, opened the cage, and, fearing that he would be punished, ran away into the woods with Iron John, who became
the child's mentor. Iron John taught him about nature and
even took him to a crystal-clear spring, telling him to guard
it and allow nothing to fall into it. On three different occasions the boy failed the test: when he dipped a wounded
finger into the spring; when a single hair off his head fell
into it; and finally, when he leaned his body over too close
to the water and all his hair fell in and turned the color of
gold. Iron John made him leave the forest to learn about

people and poverty but promised the boy that he would always help him; to receive help, the boy only had to come to the edge of the forest and yell for him. In this period, which Bly calls "the descent to ashes," the boy did lowly chores in the kitchen of a king's castle. One time he was sent to carry food to the royal table, and he refused to take off his cap that hid his golden hair. The king ordered him to be fired and to leave the castle, but the cook sent him to work in the garden. War swept the kingdom where the boy lived, and with the help of his mentor he became a successful warrior, defeated the king's enemies, married the king's daughter, found his parents, and as a result of his actions, Iron John was freed from an enchantment that had turned him into the Wild Man.

Using that story as a basis, Bly comments on the state of modern masculinity from a perspective influenced by mythology, poetry, and Jung's paradigms of the human psyche. In addition, Bly shows us the road that we should follow to become new men. According to Bly, we can recapture the positive side of our masculinity if we come in contact with our grief, which causes the absence or separation of the father. "Stealing the key, the path of ashes, the descent, coming out to the courtyard," and the change to a warrior are stages of the process to be followed in order to move into "the father's house." The warrior defines himself through his self-sacrifice and his orientation to serve. Throughout the entire process, our guide and mentor will be the Wild Man. According to Bly, "the aim is not to *be* the Wild Man, but to be *in touch with him*" (227). Looking for the Wild Man within us, we find and incorporate his qualities: spontaneity; ecological awareness and the subsequent link with nature; the ability to honor grief; and respect toward taking risks. As we delve deeper into this process of finding the Wild Man within us, we find a masculinity that is different from the oppressive and destructive man and from the tamed man. We become beings who are able not only to establish ties of cooperation and friendship with other men but also to provide nurture. The process also prepares us to find "the feminine" in its nonmaternal state.

Keen begins from an anecdotal perspective in order to describe how we become men, discusses the elements that constitute masculinity, and offers some guidelines for our transformation. The book is composed of five parts. In the first part, the author argues for the need to separate ourselves from the world of women to be able to begin the search for our own selves, a process that he calls the "invitation to a journey." In the second part, he presents other initiation rites to modern manhood, which he articulates with war, work, and sex to state that these "impoverish and alienate men" (Keen 1992, 7). Keen says that the male mind-set is a warrior psyche because society demands that we constantly resort to power and violence. "The capacity and willingness for violence has [sic] been central to our self-definition" (37). Our incorporation into the economic order makes us beings who are very competitive, oriented toward success, and subject to what the market requires of us (65). The alienation of men is a central subject for Keen, and he attributes that alienation to the fact that our lives lack meaning. Throughout the book, Keen discusses the relationship with the father and the emptiness that many men feel because their fathers were absent from the conferral of manhood. In the third part of the book, Keen discusses the visions of manhood in different historical periods to maintain that masculinity has always been defined by an integration into the universe and by the willingness to undertake the duties or "vocations" assigned to men (7).

After tracing a profile of masculinity, Keen dedicates the fourth part of his book to guiding us through the spiritual journey that leads us to a rebirth so that we will be able to comply with what he calls the historical challenge that modern man faces, which is "to discover a peaceful form of virility" (121). The last part of the book becomes a kind of recipe book on how to acquire this new masculinity and how to go more deeply into the process of spiritual renovation that will prepare us for the reunion with women.

In Puerto Rico, there are groups of men who are discussing the construction of masculinity and the possibilities for change, but so far, there is only one publication of these reflections (Cruz Díaz et al. 1990). Unlike Bly, this group does not argue for the possibility that the construction of masculinity might contain some positive factors that could serve as a basis for its transformation. For these associates, all men are oppressive, violent, and aggressive. As one of them states in his testimony, "I discovered that, although I am for women's lib and feminism, my process of liberation has been different. It is different from 'I' as 'Man,' who has always been an oppressor of woman, and my process of liberation does not stem from the experience of feeling oppressed, but rather from being the oppressor" (6). I share with these associates the objective of changing the masculine ideology that prevails, but I feel that their vision of masculinity is excessively partial toward oppressiveness. Not all men are violent, aggressive, and oppressive. There are also men who are understanding, loving, generous, and loyal. Among us there are also those who are weak, *mongos*, and cowards. Aggressiveness and assertiveness are not synonymous. These associates give the impression that they have a great sense of guilt and share a very simple conceptualization of what power is. They take power to be unilateral, exerted from above, and do not recognize that "power is everywhere," as Foucault states. They also do not seem to understand that male-female and same-sex relationships are influenced by complex games and forces of power in which everyone, both men and women, participates.

To conclude, changing our masculinity is a project. How can we achieve this change? Should we begin by stealing the key? Should we look for a new spirituality? Should we flagellate ourselves to atone for the crime of being men? I do not know, but I think that Bly, Keen, and my Puerto Rican colleagues, despite their good intentions, do not have the answer, and it is time to go forward.

Notes

1 Machismo

1. During the forties and fifties, Mexican movies would feature the figure of the *charro* as a symbol of masculinity. He was portrayed as a cowboy dressed in tight-fitting pants, an embroidered jacket, a white shirt with a scarf tied in a bow around the neck, and a wide-brimmed sombrero, and as a man who was brave, generous, loyal, honest, trained in the arts of war and love, and, above all, a singer. Jorge Negrete, actor and singer, especially of Mexican *rancheras* and *corridos*, starred in many of these movies and became one of the main *charro* actors.

2. The term did exist previous to these dates and is found in the documents of the Puerto Rican humorist and journalist Nemesio Canales. In an article originally published in 1922, Canales says: "Our brutal and loud-mouthed machismo—which sees in all women a doll without a soul or responsibility, condemned to bear us in silence, whether sister or daughter, whether girlfriend or lover or wife—continues impassively governing our life, specifying the line of conduct we must observe in any crisis in which a woman is found to be involved" (1974, 120).

3. In Puerto Rico *cafre* is used to describe anyone who behaves in a manner that is considered vulgar, in bad taste, or scandalous. The word also has a racist connotation because it is mostly applied to black people or those with physical traits considered negroid.

4. According to Stycos, "Percentages are based on the number of respondents. Since most respondents cited more than one characteristic, percentages total more than 100" (1955, 34).

5. With respect to this point, Thorn says, "Worship of the male genitals antedates all other idolatry. It can be traced to the very ancient Semitic peoples: the Assyrians, Phoenicians, Canaanites, and Midianites. Ba'al, the Sun God with generative and productive powers, was worshiped, among others, as Ba'al-Peor at a phallic altar, where naked maidens would offer themselves to worshipers in votive fornication. As the generator of all living things, Ba'al

was represented first as a detached phallus, then as an androgynous figure" (1990, 53).

6. Including Cortada de Kohan (1970), Díaz-Guerrero (1966), Díaz-Guerrero and Lara Tapia (1972), Giraldo (1972), Lewis (1966a, 1966b), Ramos (1962), and Stycos (1955).

7. "Taso" refers to the history of the life of a Puerto Rican farmer published by Sidney W. Mintz (1974). In this history, Taso narrates the most important events in his childhood and adult life: poverty, oppression, and the living and working conditions in the sugarcane area from his birth until the 1950s. "In the year 1908, at the age of 10 months, I was left fatherless with my mother, one sister, and two brothers" (27). Thus begins the life of a man who always struggles to survive and provide food for the family into which he was born. In his history there is no obsession with virility, aggressiveness, and other typical machismo traits.

8. A diplomat and Dominican playboy who married many rich and famous women. He is credited with a number of amorous conquests and having great sexual prowess. The media made him the sexual personification of the Latin man.

9. Illich makes a distinction between gender, which he calls the vernacular gender, and sex. Vernacular gender is a language through which the human species establishes complementary relationships in which the boundaries of the male and the female in relationships are marked—boundaries that are not essentially antagonistic or oppressive. Illich says, "I have adopted this term to designate a distinction in behavior, a distinction universal in vernacular cultures. It distinguishes places, times, tools, tasks, forms of speech, gestures, and perceptions that are associated with men from those associated with women. This association constitutes *social* gender because it is specific to a time and place. I call it vernacular gender because this set of associations is as peculiar to a traditional people (in Latin, *gens*) as is their vernacular speech" (1982, 3). For Illich, sex belongs to the world of scarcity and of economic growth. "By economic, or social, sex, I mean the duality that stretches toward the illusory goal of economic, political, legal, or social equality between women and men. Under this second construction of reality, as I shall show, equality is mostly fanciful" (20).

Illich's proposals have been criticized by Brittan (1989), who considers them androcentric and directed toward men. I do not agree with that criticism.

2 *The Construction of Masculinity*

1. Other authors, known as essentialists, maintain that objective and intrinsic facts exist about people's sexual orientations. A good dis-

cussion of this controversy can be found in Ruse (1988) and Stein (1992).

2. McIntosh's article was originally published in 1968.

3. This debate consists of two topics. The first one revolves around the significance of hunting in the evolution of society. During the seventies, models of evolution of hominid societies proposed what is known in the literature of anthropology as the "hunting hypothesis" (Fox 1967; Lee and De Vore 1968; Sahlins 1960; Washburn 1961). According to this hypothesis, hunting is both an activity that distinguishes our species from other hominids and specifically human and masculine. Hunting is understood as chasing, killing, and eating animals through the use of instruments. In this model, females are assigned the tasks of gathering vegetables, fruits, and roots—the argument being that menstruation, pregnancy, and lactation render them unable to hunt. Subsequently, the discovery that chimpanzees hunt, in the same way the Agta of the Philippines do (Eskioto-Griffin 1985), in which both sexes participate, plus feminist anthropologists' critiques have led to reinterpretations of the hunting society model and women's function in that model (Fedigan 1986; Mukohopadhyay and Higgins 1988; Testart 1988). In reply, Gilmore (1990) points out that hunting by Agta women has been exaggerated and that they only hunted under extreme circumstances.

The second topic is the questioning of the model of egalitarian societies, which has been generally accepted in anthropology. This model is based on an evolutionary scheme that postulates the existence of a primitive egalitarian community that develops inequality through evolutionary differentiation. This model is used by Leacock (1978) to analyze the rise of inequalities in gender relations. Those who question this model, such as Collier and Rosaldo (1981) and Flanagan (1989), stress the need to reconsider what is understood by equality and point out that the division between genders creates an inequality or asymmetry. As Flanagan says, "(even in the instances where the notion of equality could be sustained), [egalitarianism] was an egalitarianism of men" (253).

4. Gilmore's analysis will obviously not be well received by people who do not realize that masculine ideologies can contribute to the well-being of society and especially not by those who know nothing of ethnography. Stoler (1992) necessarily recognizes that Gilmore does not deal with the topic of violence against women. Although most of us in the field of anthropology do not accept, as appears in the literature on machismo, that a "quasi-natural" aggressiveness exists in men and that aggressiveness is synonymous with virility, we also do not deny the evidence that indicates that men tend to be more violent than women. This does not mean that women do not resort to violence but that ethnographic

evidence shows that even in the most egalitarian societies, men
are more prone to using violence than women. In addition, there
is conclusive evidence of rapes as acts of physical aggression against
women in many societies (Mukohopadhyay and Higgins 1988, 470).
5. A review of the state of sexuality studies from the anthropological
perspective can be found in Davis and Whitten (1987).
6. These are filiation groups formed by the descendants of a common ancestor. Clans are those groups whose members cannot specifically show who is the common ancestor, who could be real or
mythical. Lineages are groups of unilineal descendants, called
"patrilineages" or "matrilineages," depending on to whom they
trace descent, whom they know and can demonstrate as common
ancestor. As the lineages grow larger and larger in the number of
members, they separate into branches or segments.
7. This practice has been reported in other groups from New Guinea
(Herdt 1981) and is described in the fourth chapter of this book.

3 We the Boricuas

Puerto Ricans are also called Boricuas and Borinqueños. The terms
are derivations of the name the Taíno Indians gave to the island.
1. A Puerto Rican equivalent is *Dos jueyes machos no caben en una
misma cueva* (two male crabs don't fit in one hole). *Trans.*
2. I am not stating that incest does not exist in Puerto Rico. As in
other societies, people violate the ban. For an analysis of this subject, see González Knudson (1981).
3. In the city of Cayey and in other places in Puerto Rico, men call
the vegetable known as chayote (*Sechium edule*) *mujer propia*
(one's wife) "because they don't taste like nothin'." Personal com-
munication with Dr. Juan José Baldrich and Mrs. Nereida
Rodríguez.
4. Some significant studies that analyze sexual harassment and violence against women have been made by the Center for Women's
Studies, Resources and Services (known as CERES in its Spanish
acronym) under the Social Research Center of the Río Piedras Campus of the University of Puerto Rico, and in particular the publications by Martínez and Silva Bonilla (1988); Silva Bonilla (1985);
and Silva Bonilla et al. (1990).
5. In a recent study among university students on sex and knowledge of preventive measures to reduce the risk of contamination
by the human immunodeficiency virus (HIV), Cunningham
(Cunningham and Rodríguez Sánchez 1991) found what she considered to be a high frequency of anal intercourse, among both
men and women, and the infrequent use of condoms. The main
reasons the students gave for practicing anal sex were curiosity
and pleasure. Cunningham also found that the men made the de-

cision to have heterosexual anal coitus and adds, "The most frequent reason given by women for having anal intercourse is to please her partner, not for her own pleasure or to avoid becoming pregnant" (168). Owing to the lack of studies on sexuality in Puerto Rico, no conclusions can be drawn about the preference for anal sex, but it is known that here, as in the rest of the Caribbean, prominent buttocks in both women and young men are erotic objects. In *Tieta the Goat Girl* and *The War of the Saints*, Jorge Amado highlights some of the characters' likings for anal sex.

6. In U.S. culture, "getting fucked" also means to be abused, and "to fuck" means to dominate or have the advantage over another (Pronger 1990, 137). Its use is very widespread, both among men and women, at public events. The meaning of "to fuck" is practically identical to Puerto Rico's *clavar*. In the United States another verb is also used, "to screw," which has a metonymic similarity to *clavar*. The term also has a violent connotation.

7. A situation of disorder, confusion, or trouble, in short, a situation that is not clear or well defined, is known as a *crical* or *un arroz con culo* (an unholy mess).

8. Although women do not speak in this manner, some do use it, and when they are bothered, they say they are *encojonadas*, repeating the masculine discourse. Some feminists use a varied expression and say they are *ovariadas*.

9. This assertion needs to be qualified because some women urinate standing up, such as women who live in rural areas and who are from working-class backgrounds in the Puerto Rico of many decades ago. The Cuban writer Reinaldo Arenas recounts in his autobiography (1992) that his grandmother who lived in a rural area urinated standing up. The articulation of power with urinating standing up can be illustrated in graffiti that I saw in July 1991 on a wall in Caracas, Venezuela, that said, *Mujer, libérate, mea pará* (Women, free yourselves. Pee standing up). Some homosexuals urinate sitting down.

10. Act No. 83 (approved on May 31, 1972). This act amends article 263 of the Puerto Rico Penal Code. The paragraph reads, "Any parent who wilfully omits, without lawful excuse, to perform on the obligation imposed upon him by law to provide food for his children shall be guilty of a misdemeanor" (Ostolaza Bey 1989, 172).

11. Known as WIC, it is a food program for infants up to children who are five years old.

12. A job in which the risk surpasses the value that society attributes to adventure and power.

13. For generations, Puerto Ricans have been raised under the slogan "Men don't cry." Society now accepts a man who cries in public during extremely painful situations but does not accept just any

incident or even crying frequently. Should a man cry frequently, he is called a *llorón*, which is not considered manly.

14. As an example, we may point to the time when women from our society were prohibited from participating in political processes, voting, and running for elective seats. At that time, men competed among themselves in a process belonging to the sphere of masculinity. With the incorporation of women into political life, this activity loses its male exclusivity and becomes an activity shared by the two genders. In this situation, as in others in which women occupy positions that in the past were in the domain of maleness, it is necessary to question what happens to that masculine subjectivity. Is the woman desexualized? Is she considered another opponent and treated as if she were a man? Does it become acceptable for women to compete against men? These questions and others can only be answered by studies aimed at clarifying this matter.

15. Showing fear is only acceptable when death is imminent, especially on the deathbed, and showing fear of God.

16. The discussion of the cultural subject of respect is based on the works of Buitrago Ortiz (1973), Díaz Royo (1975), Lauria (1964), Manners (1956), Mintz (1956), Seda Bonilla (1957), and Wolf (1956).

17. As an example of this assertion, I cite from my field notes in a Mexican restaurant in San Juan, Puerto Rico, written on Sunday, April 8, 1979. The restaurant is very popular because of the quality of its food and is in a remodeled house in the Puerto Nuevo sector. It has a room with grillwork on the windows that faces the street, another with air-conditioning, a bar along the back wall, and 16 tables, all occupied when I entered. I waited for a table to be free. While I was eating, 12 men dressed in baseball uniforms arrived with women and children. Some of the men in uniform had shirts with *Parque de las Fuentes* written across them. These men would yell at the others, "You're from Montebello." The group took up six tables: three tables together, two others together, and one table apart. The men spoke to each other from one table to another and threw wads of paper made from the napkins on the tables at each other. The group was composed of white men in their thirties and a mulatto whom they called "Lola." When Lola went to the men's bathroom, the others would yell, "That's not it" and would signal for him to go into the women's. When he came out of the bathroom, the others yelled in unison, "Lola, Lola." The mulatto laughed and walked with a swing in his hips. One of the men went to the bathroom, followed by another a few minutes later. When they came out together, a male voice from one of the tables occupied by the group asked them, "What were you two doing in there?" At the table in front of mine, one of the men sat on the lap of another and hugged him. The others began to laugh

and yell. A man from another table rose and covered the head of one of the hugging men with a tablecloth, and then he said to one of the waiters, "Find a priest to marry them." The women smiled and hardly spoke at all. The men continued talking among themselves while drinking beer or tequila and continued throwing wads of paper from one table to another. I left the restaurant before they were served their lunch.

4 *The Homosexual Question*

1. Homosexuality has also been reported among animals. Regarding this subject, Ruse states, "We know that in species after species, right through the animal kingdom, students of animal behaviour report unambiguous evidence of homosexual attachments and behaviour—in insects, fish, birds, and lower and higher mammals" (1988, 189). Additional evidence appears in Denniston (1980) and Weinrich (1982).

2. An extensive examination of the literature on homosexuality in different societies appears in Greenberg (1988). He points out that for several decades of this century, anthropologists tended to avoid homosexuality and not investigate how it was expressed. For some anthropologists, homosexuality was unrelated to the purposes of their field research. In other cases, the anthropologist's homophobia or the taboo regarding discussion of homosexuality in academic circles may have been a factor that explains why such practices were not reported. In addition, it is necessary to consider that homoeroticism may have been kept secret because of its association with rituals or because the native subjects were aware of its rejection by the missionaries and colonial administrators. In the case of Herdt (1981), the author of an extensive study of a New Guinea society, homoeroticism was so secretive that it took the anthropologist many months to be able to observe the rituals associated with the practice.

3. Regarding this aspect, Pronger says, "Viewed objectively, any sexual act involving persons of the same physical sex can be considered a homosexual act. But the simple physical fact of a man's penis being in another man's hand, mouth or anus is, in itself, insignificant. In our culture, there is great import attached to our saying that someone has been involved in homosexuality. What the homosexual act might mean to those involved, to someone who suspects another of being homosexual, can be highly significant" (1990, 6).

4. Although I prefer the term "homoeroticism" because it does not have the negative connotation or the clinical meaning of homosexuality, I shall use the term "homosexuality" to place myself within its widespread use in the literature of this aspect of male

sexuality. The importance of studying and discussing homosexuality in academic circles in the United States and some European countries is seen in publications following the important works of Tripp (1975) and Dover (1978), parts of which are cited in this book. Two excellent journals are the *Journal of Homosexuality* and the *Journal of the History of Sexuality*. Recently, the *Chronicle of Higher Education* published an article (McMillen 1992) that reviewed the current importance being given to gay and lesbian studies, as seen in the subjects of dissertations and their publication by important university presses.

5. In a summary of ethnographic evidence, Greenberg says, "In some groups, male berdaches hunted and fought, though they wore men's clothing when they did so. Male berdaches of the Pima and Navaho were not required to cross-dress. In a number of groups, they did both men's and women's work" (1988, 42).

6. Foucault's original version in French was published in 1984. Cf. also Greenberg (1988) and Keuls (1985); both contain excellent bibliographies.

7. A beautiful youth with whom Zeus falls in love. The god changes into an eagle, kidnaps Ganymede, and takes him to Mount Olympus. The versions and transformations of the myth may be found in Keuls (1985).

8. Lewis questions this situation when he says, "We shall never know the nature of trangressions of the law, and we shall never know what was silently tolerated in everyday life. Should we believe, as law and custom would have us do, that a young, pubescent *eromenos* took no physical pleasure from the actions of his *erastes*?" (1982, 159–160).

9. Herdt (1981) warns that some married men continue preferring homoerotic relations and practice them, although society rejects them for doing so. Most men make the transition to complete heterosexuality (252).

10. As part of the evidence against Wilde, the following poem by his friend Lord Alfred Douglas was cited during the trial. The opposition of Alfred's father to his relationship with Wilde was one of the leading causes of the accusation and the trial.

    Two Loves
    Sweet youth,
    Tell me shy, sad and sighing, dost thou rove
    These pleasant realms? I pray thee tell me sooth,
    What is thy name? He said, "My name is love,"
    Then straight the first did turn himself to me,
    And cried, "He lieth, for his name is Shame.
    But I am Love, and I was wont to be
    Alone in this fair garden, till he came
    Unasked by night: I am true Love, I fill
    The hearths of boy and girl with mutual flame."

Then sighing said the other, "Have thy will,
I am the Love that dare not speak its name."

11. In Western thought, believing sexual intercourse between men to be unnatural can be traced back to Plato. The medieval debate over sodomy and its changing conceptions are widely discussed in Greenberg (1988), Boswell (1980), Hyde (1970), and Illich (1982).

12. In 1974, by a vote of 5,845 to 3,810, the American Psychiatric Association stopped classifying homosexuality as a psychological dysfunction (Bayer 1981), and the categories of ego-dystonic homosexuality (homosexuals with psychological problems caused by their sexual preference) and ego-syntonic homosexuality (those adapted to their sexual orientation) were incorporated into the Diagnostic and Statistical Manual (DSM III). This distinction was eliminated in the revised manual published in 1985 (Jorge-Rivera 1989, 9).

13. A detailed analysis of the debate and of the possibility that homosexuality is innate and the various explanations of its biology may be found in Greenberg (1988, 409–437) and Ruse (1988, 84–175).

14. García Córdova's research (1984) among students of the University of Puerto Rico, Río Piedras Campus, indicates the variation that exists between acceptance and rejection. Research on the subject of homosexuality in Puerto Rican society is very scarce and is mainly limited to student theses. In addition to García Córdova, the works of Casper Quiñones (1971), Firpi Samper (1977), Garrido Cole (1976), González Gelabert (1989, 1991), Jorge-Rivera (1989), Ortiz Colón (1991), Rosario Collazo (1984), and Sosa Peña (1981) are included in the bibliography at the end of the book.

15. Act No. 115 of July 22, 1974, of the Penal Code, approved by the Puerto Rico legislature, states that sexual intercourse between persons of the same sex constitutes a crime against decency and is considered to be sodomy: "Article 103—Any person who has sexual intercourse with a person of the same sex or commits the crime against nature with a human being, shall be punished by imprisonment for a fixed term of ten (10) years. Under aggravating circumstances, the established term of punishment may be increased to a maximum of twelve (12) years; under extenuating circumstances, the term may be reduced to a minimum of six (6) years."

16. The term *pato* (duck) is used as a synonym for *maricón* when the speaker feels that *maricón* sounds too strong, gross, or vulgar. The term "homosexual" has yet a more technical connotation and is accepted as respectable by the arbiters of good speech in Puerto Rico.

17. There are persons who have been raised in this religious environment and have rejected it to join *el ambiente*. Others participate in *el ambiente* occasionally, which conflicts with their religious beliefs and causes them a great sense of guilt.

18. Pronger's (1990) analysis of this phenomenon, which he calls a homoerotic paradox, is similar to mine.
19. This word is always used in English, and there is no equivalent word in Spanish.
20. The term "closet" is always used in English.
21. Calling somebody a "closet queen" is considered to be insulting or at least derogatory. In *el ambiente*, the *loca de closet* is rejected because he is a person who does not inspire trust and is considered to be a coward for not accepting his sexuality. He is suspected of being homophobic and is offended because his hopes of claiming masculinity are not recognized.
22. Some say they like their men the way they like their coffee: black, sweet, hot, and strong.
23. The fear of being contaminated by the AIDS virus and the high crime rate are factors contributing to fewer casual sexual encounters between people who are very removed from the class structure.
24. With respect to its use in the United States, Herdt states that "as a category ["gay"] is not prominent in popular discourse until the late 1950s and early 1960s (though gay novelists such as Edmund White make it seem prevalent earlier). By the 1970s, it was increasingly common; by the 1980s, it was canonical in the gay cultural system" (1992, 4).
25. Located in Greenwich Village in New York City, Stonewall Inn was a bar frequented by homosexuals; it was raided by city police as part of a pattern of persecution of alternative sexualities. On the night of June 29, 1969, bar patrons responded spontaneously to the police attack. The confrontation between the two camps ended in a riot that has gone down in history as the event that catalyzed the gay movement. Many people involved were Puerto Rican transvestites.
26. A popular slogan in the United States was "Out of the closets and into the streets."
27. This movement's history has been analyzed by Negrón-Muntaner (1992).
28. It is possible that part of this fear is linked to the possibility of enjoying being penetrated. I argue this as a hypothesis.

Bibliography

Abad, V., J. Ramos, and E. Boyce. 1974. "A Model for the Delivery of Mental Health Services to Spanish Speaking Minorities." *American Journal of Orthopsychiatry* 44: 584–595.

Arenas, Reinaldo. 1992. *Antes que anochezca: Autobiografía*. Barcelona: Tusquet Editores, S.A.

Azize Vargas, Yamila., et al. 1992. *Hacia un currículo no sexista*. Cayey: University of Puerto Rico, Cayey University College, Women's Studies Project.

Bayer, R. 1981. *Homosexuality and American Psychiatry*. New York: Basic Books.

Benedict, Ruth. 1946. *Patterns of Culture*. New York: Mentor Books.

Bermúdez, M. E. 1955. "La vida familiar del mexicano." *México y lo mexicano*, no. 20. México: Antigua Librería Robredo.

Bieber, Irving. 1965. "Clinical Aspects of Male Homosexuality." In *Sexual Inversion: The Multiple Roots of Homosexuality*, edited by Judd Marmor, 248–267. New York: Basic Books.

Bird Piñero, Enrique. 1991. *Don Luis Muñoz Marín: El poder de la excelencia*. San Juan: Fundación Luis Muñoz Marín.

Blok, Anton. 1981. "Rams and Billy-Goats: A Key to the Mediterranean Code of Honour." *Man* 16:427–440.

Bly, Robert. 1990. *Iron John: A Book about Men*. Reading, Mass.: Addison-Wesley Publishing Co.

Boswell, John. 1980. *Christianity, Social Tolerance, and Homosexuality*. Chicago: University of Chicago Press.

———. 1992. "Categories, Experience, and Sexuality." In *Forms of Desire: Sexual Orientation and the Social Constructionist Controversy*, edited by Edward Stein, 133–173. New York: Routledge.

Brandes, Stanley H. 1980. *Metaphors of Masculinity: Sex and Status in Andalusian Folklore*. Philadelphia: University of Pennsylvania Press.

———. 1981. "Like Wounded Stags: Male Sexual Ideology in an Andalusian Town." In *Sexual Meanings: The Cultural Construction of Gender and Sexuality*, edited by Sherry B. Ortner and Harriet Whitehead, 216–239. Cambridge: Cambridge University Press.

Brittan, Arthur. 1989. *Masculinity and Power*. Oxford: Basil Blackwell.

Buitrago Ortiz, Carlos. 1973. *Esperanza: An Ethnographic Study of a Peasant Community in Puerto Rico*. Viking Fund Publications in Anthropology, no. 50. Tucson: University of Arizona Press.

Burgos, Nilsa M., and Eileen Colberg. 1990. *Mujeres solteras con jefatura de familia: Características en el hogar y en el trabajo*. Río Piedras: University of Puerto Rico, Center for Social Research.

Campbell, J. K. 1966. "Honour and the Devil." In *Honour and Shame: The Values of Mediterranean Society*, edited by J. G. Peristiany, 139–170. Chicago: University of Chicago Press.

Canales, Nemesio R. 1974. "Nuestro machismo." In *Antología nueva de Canales*, edited by Servando Montaña, 2:119–124. Río Piedras, Puerto Rico: Editorial Universitaria.

Carnivalli, Judith, and Irma Rivera. 1991. "Las muertes violentas en Puerto Rico." Unpublished manuscript.

Casper Quiñones, W. T. 1971. "La homosexualidad latente y su inaceptabilidad en los hombres paranoides según el modelo freudiano." Master's thesis, Psychology Department, Río Piedras Campus, University of Puerto Rico.

Clifford, James, and George E. Marcus, eds. 1986. *Writing Culture: The Poetics and Politics of Ethnography*. Berkeley and Los Angeles: University of California Press.

Collier, Jane F., and Michelle Z. Rosaldo. 1981. "Politics and Gender in Simple Societies." In *Sexual Meanings: The Cultural Construction of Gender and Sexuality*, edited by Sherry B. Ortner and Harriet Whitehead, 275–329. Cambridge: Cambridge University Press.

Cortada de Kohan, Nuria. 1970. "Un estudio experimental del machismo." *Revista Latinoamericana de Psicología* 2 (1): 33–56.

Cruz Díaz, Edwin, et al. 1990. *Relexiones en torno a la ideología y vivencia masculina*. Río Piedras: University of Puerto Rico, Center for Social Research.

Cunningham, Ineke, and Mario H. Rodríguez Sánchez. 1991. "Prácticas de riesgo relacionadas con la transmisión del VIH y medidas de prevención entre estudiantes de la Universidad de Puerto Rico: 1989 and 1990." In *El Sida en Puerto Rico: Acercamientos multidisciplinarios*, edited by Ineke Cunningham, Carlos G. Ramos Bellido, and Reinaldo Ortiz Colón, 147–173. Río Piedras: University of Puerto Rico, Institute of Caribbean Studies.

Davis, D. L., and R. G. Whitten. 1987. "The Cross-Cultural Study of Human Sexuality." *Annual Review of Anthropology* 16:69–98.

De Jesús Guerrero, Manuel. 1977. *El machismo latinoamericano*. New York: Plus Ultra Educational Publishers.

De Jesús Mangual, Tomás. 1984. "Mata amigo le 'falta el respeto.'" *El Vocero*, March 26.

———. 1992. "Acusan madre restrella bebé contra su cunita." *El Vocero*, October 6.

De la Cancela, Víctor. 1981. "Towards a Critical Psychological Analysis of Machismo: Puerto Ricans and Mental Health." Ph.D. diss., City University of New York.

Denniston, R. M. 1980. "Ambisexuality in Animals." In *Homosexual Behaviour: A Modern Reappraisal*, edited by J. Marmor, 25–40. New York: Basic Books.

Díaz-Guerrero, Rogelio. 1966. *Estudios de psicología del mexicano*. México: Ediciones Trillas.

Díaz-Guerrero, Rogelio, and Luis Lara Tapia. 1972. "Diferencias sexuales en el desarrollo de la personalidad del escolar mexicano." *Revista Latinoamericana de Psicología* 4 (3): 345–351.

Díaz Royo, Antonio T. 1975. "The Enculturation Process of Puerto Rican Highland Children." Ph.D. diss., State University of New York at Albany.

Dover, K. J. 1978. *Greek Homosexuality*. Cambridge: Harvard University Press.

Epstein, Steven. 1992. "Gay Politics, Ethnic Identity: The Limits of Social Constructionism." In *Forms of Desire: Sexual Orientation and the Social Constructionist Controversy*, edited by Edward Stein, 239–293. New York: Routledge.

Eskioto-Griffin, Agnes. 1985. "Women as Hunters: The Case of an Eastern Cagayan Agta Group." In *The Agta of Northeastern Luzorn: Recent Studies*, edited by P. Bion Griffin and Agnes Eskioto-Griffin, 18–32. Cebu City, Philippines: San Carlos Publishers.

Esteves, José. 1992. "Ellos viven de sus cuerpos." Television report on male prostitution.

Fausto-Sterling, Anne. 1985. *Myths of Gender: Biological Theories about Men and Women*. New York: Basic Books.

Fedigan, Linda Marie. 1986. "The Changing Role of Women in Models of Human Evolution." *Annual Review of Anthropology* 15:25–66.

Firpi Samper, M. 1977. "Constructos personales y orientación interna-externa en dos grupos de homosexuales puertorriqueños." Master's thesis, Psychology Department, Río Piedras Campus, University of Puerto Rico.

Flanagan, James G. 1989. "Hierarchy in Simple 'Egalitarian' Societies." *Annual Review of Anthropology* 18:245–266.

Foucault, Michel. 1990a. *The History of Sexuality*. Vol. 1, *An Introduction*. Translated by Robert Hurley. New York: Vintage-Random.

———. 1990b. *The History of Sexuality*. Vol. 2, *The Use of Pleasure*. Translated by Robert Hurley. New York: Vintage-Random.

Fox, Robin. 1967. "In the Beginning: Aspects of Hominid Behavioural Evolution." *Man* 2 (3): 415–433.

Friedl, Ernestine. 1975. *Women and Men: An Anthropologist's View*. New York: Holt, Rinehart and Winston.

García Córdova, Héctor J. 1984. "Actitudes hacia los homosexuales y lesbianas de cuatro grupos de estudiantes universitarios." Master's thesis, Psychology Department, Río Piedras Campus, University of Puerto Rico.

García Passalacqua, Juan Manuel. 1990. *Casa sin hogar: Memoria de mis tiempos: Puerto Rico, 1937–1987.* Río Piedras, Puerto Rico: Editorial Edil.

Garrido Cole, M. 1976. "Sexual Identification in Male Heroin Addicts." Master's thesis, Psychology Department, Río Piedras Campus, University of Puerto Rico.

Geertz, Clifford. 1973. *The Interpretation of Cultures.* New York: Basic Books.

Gilmore, David D. 1990. *Manhood in the Making: Cultural Concepts of Masculinity.* New Haven: Yale University Press.

Giraldo, Octavio. 1972. "El machismo como fenómeno psico-cultural." *Revista Latinoamericana de Psicología* 4 (3): 295–309.

Godelier, Maurice. 1986. *The Making of Great Men: Male Domination and Power among the New Guinea Baruya.* Translated by Rubert Swyer. Cambridge: Cambridge University Press.

González Gelabert, María. 1989. "Construcción ideológica del SIDA por tres varones homosexuales: Un estudio descriptivo en Puerto Rico." Master's thesis, Psychology Department, Río Piedras Campus, University of Puerto Rico.

———. 1991. "El SIDA y la homosexualidad: Apuntes para la intervención psicoterapéutica o la consejería." In *EL SIDA en Puerto Rico: Acercamientos multidisciplinarios,* edited by Ineke Cunningham, Carlos G. Ramos Bellido, and Reinaldo Ortiz Colón, 231–239. Río Piedras: University of Puerto Rico, Institute of Caribbean Studies.

González Knudson, Doris. 1981. "Interpersonal Dynamics and Mother's Involvement in Father-Daughter Incest in Puerto Rico." Ph.D. diss., Ohio State University.

Greenberg, David F. 1988. *The Construction of Homosexuality.* Chicago: University of Chicago Press.

Griffin, Jasper. 1990. "Love and Sex in Greece." *The New York Review of Books* 37 (5): 6–12.

Herdt, Gilbert H. 1981. *Guardians of the Flutes: Idioms of Masculinity.* New York: McGraw Hill.

———, ed. 1982. *Rituals of Manhood: Male Initiation in Papua New Guinea.* Berkeley and Los Angeles: University of California Press.

———, ed. 1992. *Gay Culture in America: Essays from the Field.* Boston: Beacon Press.

Herzfeld, Michael. 1985. *The Poetics of Manhood: Contest and Identity in a Cretan Mountain Village.* Princeton, N.J.: Princeton University Press.

Hill, Reuben, J. Mayone Stycos, and Kurt W. Back. 1959. *The Family and Population Control: A Puerto Rican Experiment in Social Change.* Chapel Hill: University of North Carolina Press.

Hyde, H. Montgomery. 1970. *The Love That Dared Not Speak Its Name: A Candid History of Homosexuality in Britain.* Boston: Little, Brown and Co.

Illich, Ivan. 1982. *Gender.* New York: Pantheon-Random.

Jorge-Rivera, Juan Carlos. 1989. "Formación y transformación de la identidad homosexual: Historia de vida de un hombre puertorriqueño." Honor's thesis, Honors Program, Río Piedras Campus, University of Puerto Rico.

Keen, Sam. 1992. *Fire in the Belly: On Being a Man.* New York: Bantam Books.

Keuls, Eva C. 1985. *The Reign of Phallus: Sexual Politics in Ancient Greece.* New York: Harper & Row.

Kluckhohn, Clyde. 1957. *Mirror for Man.* Greenwich, Conn.: Fawcett Publications.

Konner, Melvin. 1982. *The Tangled Wing: Biological Constraints on the Human Spirit.* New York: Harper Colophon Books.

Kutsche, Paul, and J. Bryan Page. 1992. "Male Sexual Identity in Costa Rica." *The Latin American Anthropology Review* 3 (1): 7–14.

Landy, David. 1965. *Tropical Childhood: Cultural Transmission and Learning in a Rural Puerto Rican Village.* New York: Harper.

Lauria, Anthony, Jr. 1964. "'Respeto,' 'Relajo' and Interpersonal Relations in Puerto Rico." *Anthropological Quarterly* 3:53–67.

Leacock, Eleanor. 1978. "Women's Status in Egalitarian Society: Implications for Social Evolution." *Current Anthropology* 19 (2): 247–275.

Lee, Richard B., and Irving De Vore, eds. 1968. *Man the Hunter.* Chicago: Aldine.

LeVay, Simon. 1991. "A Difference in Hypothalamic Structure between Heterosexual and Homosexual Men." *Science* 253:1034–1037.

Lewis, Oscar. 1966a. *Pedro Martínez.* México: Editorial Mortiz.

———. 1966b. *Los hijos de Sánchez.* México: Editorial Mortiz.

———. 1966c. *La vida.* New York: Random House.

Lewis, Thomas, S.W. 1982. "The Brothers of Ganymede." In *Homosexuality: Sacrilege, Vision, Politics,* edited by Robert Boyers and George Steiner, 147–165. Saratoga Springs, N.Y.: Skidmore College.

Maccoby, Eleanor, and Carol Jacklin. 1974. *The Psychology of Sex Differences.* Stanford, Calif.: Stanford University Press.

MacCormack, Carol, and Marilyn Strathern, eds. 1980. *Nature, Culture, and Gender.* Cambridge: Cambridge University Press.

McIntosh, Mary. 1992. "The Homosexual Role." In *Forms of Desire: Sexual Orientation and the Sexual Constructionist Controversy,* edited by Edward Stein, 25–42. New York: Routledge.

McMillen, Liz. 1992. "From Margin to Mainstream: Books in Gay and Lesbian Studies." *Chronicle of Higher Education* 38 (46): A8–9, 13.

Manners, Robert A. 1956. "Tabara: Subcultures of a Tobacco and Mixed

Crops Municipality." In *The People of Puerto Rico: A Study in Social Anthropology*, edited by Julian H. Steward, 93–170. Urbana: University of Illinois Press.

Marcus, George E., and Michael M. J. Fischer. 1986. *Anthropology as Cultural Critique: An Experimental Moment in the Human Sciences*. Chicago: University of Chicago Press.

Martínez, Lourdes, and Ruth Silva Bonilla. 1988. *El hostigamiento sexual de las trabajadoras en sus centros de empleo*. Río Piedras: University of Puerto Rico, Center for Social Research.

Masters, William H., and Virginia E. Johnson. 1966. *Human Sexual Response*. Boston: Little, Brown and Co.

Mead, Margaret. 1950. *Sex and Temperament in Three Primitive Societies*. New York: Mentor.

Mejía Ricart, Tirso. 1975. "Observaciones sobre el machismo en la América Latina." *Revista de Ciencias Sociales* 19 (3): 351–364.

Millán Pabón, Carmen. 1992. "Arrasa con los varones el SIDA." *El Nuevo Día*, August 18.

Mintz, Sidney W. 1956. "Cañamelar: The Subculture of a Rural Sugar Plantation Proletariat." In *The People of Puerto Rico: A Study in Social Anthropology*, edited by Julian H. Steward, 314–417. Urbana: University of Illinois Press.

———. 1974. *Worker in the Cane: A Puerto Rican Life History*. New York: W. W. Norton & Co.

Moore, Henrietta L. 1986. *Space, Text, and Gender: An Anthropological Study of the Marakwet of Kenya*. Cambridge: Cambridge University Press.

Mukohopadhyay, Carol C., and Patricia Higgins. 1988. "Anthropological Studies of Women's Status Revisited: 1977–1987." *Annual Review of Anthropology* 17: 461–495.

Nash, June. 1979. *We Eat the Mines and the Mines Eat Us: Dependency and Exploitation in Bolivian Tin Mines*. New York: Columbia University Press.

Negrón-Muntaner, Frances. 1992. "Echoing Stonewall and Other Dilemmas: The Organizational Beginnings of a Gay and Lesbian Agenda in Puerto Rico, 1972–1977." Pts. 1 and 2. *Centro de Estudios Puertorriqueños Bulletin* 4, no. 1: 76–95; no. 2: 98–115.

Ortiz Colón, Reinaldo. 1991. "Grupos de apoyo con hombres homosexuales VIH-seropositivos: Un estudio de caso en Puerto Rico." In *El SIDA en Puerto Rico: Acercamientos multidisciplinarios*, edited by Ineke Cunninghman, Carlos G. Ramos Bellido, and Reinaldo Ortiz Colón, 215–230. Río Piedras: University of Puerto Rico, Institute of Caribbean Studies.

Ortner, Sherry B., and Harriet Whitehead, eds. 1981. *Sexual Meanings: The Cultural Construction of Gender and Sexuality*. Cambridge: Cambridge University Press.

Ostolaza Bey, Margarita. 1989. *Política sexual en Puerto Rico*. Río Piedras, Puerto Rico: Ediciones Huracán.

Padilla, A. M., and R. A. Ruiz. 1973. *Latino Mental Health: A Review of Literature.* Rockville, Md.: National Institute of Mental Health.

Palés Matos, Luis. 1964. *Poesía: 1915–1956.* Río Piedras, Puerto Rico: Editorial Universitaria.

Paz, Octavio. 1961. *The Labyrinth of Solitude.* Translated by Lysander Kemp. New York: Grove Press.

Peristiany, J. G., ed. 1966. *Honour and Shame: The Values of Mediterranean Society.* Chicago: University of Chicago Press.

Picó, Fernando. 1989. *Vivir en Caimito.* Río Piedras, Puerto Rico: Ediciones Huracán.

Picó, Isabel. 1979. *Machismo y educación en Puerto Rico.* San Juan: Comisión para el Mejoramiento de los Derechos de la Mujer.

Pitt-Rivers, Julian. 1966. "Honor and Social Status." In *Honour and Shame: The Values of Mediterranean Society,* edited by J. G. Peristiany, 19–77. Chicago: University of Chicago Press.

———. 1977. *The Fate of Shechem, or the Politics of Sex: Essays in the Anthropology of the Mediterranean.* Cambridge: Cambridge University Press.

Posner, Richard A. 1992. *Sex and Reason.* Cambridge: Harvard University Press.

Pronger, Brian. 1990. *The Arena of Masculinity: Sports, Homosexuality, and the Meaning of Sex.* New York: St. Martin's Press.

Ramírez, Rafael L. 1989. "Ideologías masculinas, sexualidad y poder." Paper presented at the Twenty-second Interamerican Congress of Psychology, Buenos Aires, Argentina, June 25–30.

Ramos, Samuel. 1962. *Profile of Man and Culture in Mexico.* Austin: University of Texas Press.

Reiter, Rayna R., ed. 1975. *Toward an Anthropology of Women.* New York: Monthly Review Press.

Richmond-Abbot, Marie. 1992. *Masculine and Feminine: Gender Roles over the Life Cycle.* New York: McGraw-Hill.

Rivera Medina, Eduardo. 1991. "Poder, placer y penuria: Reflexiones en torno a la masculinidad." Interamerican Award lecture presented at the Twenty-third Interamerican Congress of Psychology, San Jose, Costa Rica, July 7–12.

Rivera Medina, Eduardo, and Rafael L. Ramírez. 1985. *Del cañaveral a la fábrica: Cambio social en Puerto Rico.* Río Piedras, Puerto Rico: Ediciones Huracán.

Rodríguez Juliá, Edgardo. 1988. *Puertorriqueños: Album de la sagrada familia puertorriqueña a partir de 1898.* Madrid: Editorial Playor.

Rosario Collazo, Wayne G. 1984. "El desarrollo de la comunidad y la promoción como vehículos liberadores ante la marginalización de la homosexualidad en una comunidad de clase media." Master's thesis, Psychology Department, University of Puerto Rico, Rio Piedras.

Ruse, Michael. 1988. *Homosexuality: A Philosophical Inquiry.* Oxford: Basil Blackwell.

Sahlins, Marshall. 1960. "The Origin of Society." *Scientific American* 203 (3): 76–86.

Sanday, Peggy Reeves. 1981. *Female Power and Male Dominance: On the Origins of Sexual Inequality.* Cambridge: Cambridge University Press.

Seda Bonilla, Eduardo. 1957. "The Normative Patterns of the Puerto Rican Family in Various Situational Contexts." Ph.D. diss., Faculty of Political Sciences, Columbia University.

Silva Bonilla, Ruth. 1985. *¡Ay! ¡Ay! amor: No me quieras tanto. (El marco social de la violencia contra la mujer en la vida conyugal).* Río Piedras: University of Puerto Rico, Center for Social Research.

Silva Bonilla, Ruth, et al. 1990. *Hay amores que matan: La violencia contra las mujeres en la vida conyugal.* Río Piedras, Puerto Rico: Ediciones Huracán.

Sosa Peña, D. M. 1981. "El estilo de vida de un grupo de homosexuales del área metropolitana de San Juan y su relación con algunas variables." Master's thesis, Psychology Department, Río Piedras Campus, University of Puerto Rico.

Stein, Edward, ed. 1992. *Forms of Desire: Sexual Orientation and the Social Constructionist Controversy.* New York: Routledge.

Stevens, E. P. 1976. "Marianismo: The Other Face of Machismo in Latin America." In *Female and Male in Latin America: Essays,* edited by A. Pescatello, 89–101. Pittsburgh: University of Pittsburgh Press.

Stoler, Ann. 1992. "Book Review." *American Anthropologist* 94 (1): 192–193.

Stone, I. F. 1974. "Machismo in Washington." In *Men and Masculinity,* edited by J. Pleck and J. Sawyer, 130–133. Englewood Cliffs, N.J.: Prentice Hall.

Stycos, J. Mayone. 1955. *Family and Fertility in Puerto Rico: A Study of the Lower Income Group.* New York: Columbia University Press.

Testart, Alain. 1988. "Some Major Problems in the Social Anthropology of Hunters-Gatherers." *Current Anthropology* 29 (1): 1–31.

Thorn, Mark. 1990. *Taboo No More: The Phallus in Fact, Fiction, and Fantasy.* New York: Shapolsky Publishers.

Tiger, Lionel. 1970. *Men in Groups.* New York: Vintage.

Tripp, C. A. 1975. *The Homosexual Matrix.* New York: McGraw-Hill.

Vanggaard, Thorkil. 1972. *Phallós: A Symbol and Its History in the Male World.* New York: International Universities Press.

Walter, Eugene Victor. 1969. *Terror and Resistance: A Study of Political Violence.* New York: Oxford University Press.

Washburn, S. L., ed. 1961. *Social Life of Early Man.* Chicago: Aldine.

Weber, Max. 1958. "Class, Status, Party." In *From Max Weber: Essays in Sociology,* edited and translated by Hans H. Gerth and C. Wright Mills, 180–195. New York: Galaxy–Oxford University Press.

Wehbe Cabanay, María Cristina. 1992. "Perfil del estudiante de los programas de maestría y doctorado: Análisis sociológico de clase y género." Master's thesis, Sociology Department, Río Piedras Campus, University of Puerto Rico.

Weinrich, J. D. 1982. "Is Homosexuality Biologically Natural?" In *Homosexuality: Social, Psychological, and Biological Issues*, edited by W. Paul, J. D. Weinrich, J. C. Gonsiorek, and M. E. Hotvedt, 197–208. Beverly Hills, Calif.: Sage.

Whitehead, Harriet. 1981. "The Bow and the Strap: A New Look at Institutionalized Homosexuality in Native North America." In *Sexual Meanings: The Cultural Construction of Gender and Sexuality*, edited by Sherry B. Ortner and Harriet Whitehead, 80–115. Cambridge: Cambridge University Press.

Williams, Raymond. 1977. *Marxism and Literature*. Oxford: Oxford University Press.

Wilson, William Julius. 1990. *The Truly Disadvantaged: The Inner City, the Underclass, and Public Policy*. Chicago: University of Chicago Press.

Wolf, Eric R. 1956. "San José: Subcultures of a Traditional Coffee Municipality." In *The People of Puerto Rico: A Study in Social Anthropology*, edited by Julian H. Steward, 171–264. Urbana: University of Illinois Press.

Wolf, Kathleen L. 1952. "Growing Up and Its Price in Three Puerto Rican Subcultures." *Psychiatry* 15 (4): 401–433.

Index

About the Author

Rafael L. Ramírez was born in San Juan, Puerto Rico. He is a retired professor of anthropology and senior researcher at the HIV/AIDS Research and Education Center at the University of Puerto Rico, Río Piedras. Major publications are *Dime capitán: reflexiones sobre la masculinidad* (1993), of which *What It Means to Be a Man* is a translation, and *El arrabal y la política* (1977). He coedited (with Eduardo Rivera Medina) *Del cañaveral a la fábrica: cambio social en Puerto Rico* (1988). Currently he is working on a research project on masculine and sexual identities in the Caribbean.

About the Translator

Rosa "Ginny" Casper began translating informally when she served as a Peace Corps volunteer in Paraguay. While completing her master's degree in translation at the University of Puerto Rico, she worked at the *San Juan Star* newspaper as a translator for the Spanish edition. She is currently an editorialist and freelance translator in the New York City area, where she lives with her husband, Peter, and their dog, Taína.